HELP FOR HELPERS

Daily Meditations for Counselors

HELP FOR HELPERS

Daily Meditations for Counselors

Hazelden
Center City, Minnesota 55012-0176

©1989 by Hazelden Foundation
All rights reserved. Previously published by
Parkside Publishing Corporation 1989. First
published by Hazelden Foundation 1994
Printed in the United States of America
No portion of this publication may be
reproduced in any manner without the
written permission of the publisher

ISBN: 978-1-56838-061-2

INTRODUCTION

This book was written by counselors, administrators, and support staff in addiction treatment centers from big cities and small towns all across the country.

On these pages, we've shared our thoughts and feelings, our ups and downs, our fears, our hopes, and our dreams. We wrote these meditations to comfort, to teach, and to challenge; to understand each other, and ourselves, a little better.

This book was written as a gift to ourselves, to each other, and to you. We hope you enjoy reading these meditations as much as we enjoyed writing them.

This is no dress rehearsal—this is it
The beginning of a new day
God has given me this day to use as I will
To waste, or to use for good.

Everything I do today counts:
I'm exchanging a day of my life for it
A day that will never come again
Tomorrow, this day will be gone forever
Leaving me whatever I have paid for it.

I want it to be gain, not loss
Good, not evil
Joy, not sorrow
Success, not failure.

When tomorrow comes
I pray not to regret the price
I paid for this day.

S.B.-P.
Houston, TX

January is a serious, no-nonsense, get-down-to-business, back-to-basics month for a counselor. I like that. After the holiday whirlwind, it's time to get quiet and take up the task of work once again.

Work. It's a simple, strong word. Work. It is a constant for me. Even when I'm playing, I'm working. I like that, too, because it brings out the best in me.

Work. It makes me sweat, tries my brain, draws me into myself, and pushes me out to others.

Work. It makes me laugh. It makes me cry. I love it.

Grant me the chance to show my love through my work today.

J.E.
Park Ridge, IL

The journey of recovery may be a long one. We emerge tired, empty, and sore. We must stop for rest, to refill ourselves. We can still taste the memories of our illness; we use them to feel the life inside us; they guide us on our chosen journey.

Next, we begin to feel the life about us. It brings many questions. Don't be afraid to ask those questions; we are all newborns. We will open our minds, our eyes, our hearts, to the perfection of our Higher Power, and will come to find the balance within.

Now begins another journey on the road of recovery; the road on which we will come to know ourselves. Have courage; with the help of our Higher Power, negative feelings will fade. In return, we will find empathy, gratitude, compassion, humility, acceptance, passion, tolerance, and forgiveness. We will know love.

Today, help me to hear the answers. Help me to feel the balance.

K.P.
Park Ridge, IL

"The wisdom to know the difference:" the shortest and last line of the Serenity Prayer holds the key to detachment.

Grant me the wisdom to separate the emotions from the event, the actions from the person.

Grant me the wisdom to remember that I'm unable to control another person or situation.

Grant me the wisdom to stay out of the way, allowing others the dignity to make their own decisions, even if those decisions are different from mine.

Grant me the wisdom to focus on my own behavior and responsibilities.

Grant me the wisdom to detach.

Grant me the wisdom to let go and let God.

E.C.
Des Plaines, IL

Like a plant that moves to face the sun, let me turn my attention to the beauty and joy of life. I know people who seem almost to look for pain and rejection. It's always there, the negatives, the disappointments, and the pain. But the beauty and wonder are always there, too, if I look for them.

Today, I want to think about the many things that inspire me, that bring goodness to my life. The joy I feel helping others. The love of family and friends. The beauty of the world around me. Help me let go of anger and pain. Help me to resist the temptation of self-pity. Let me be persistent, and not be discouraged when life gets complicated and tasks are hard to complete. Like that plant, help me to keep trying to find the sun.

Anonymous

Living in fear can be just as debilitating as living in active addiction. Fear is the father of anger and self-pity, and if allowed to go unchecked, will wreak havoc on ourselves as well as our loved ones.

It's said that trust is the opposite of fear—not simply trust in ourselves, but complete trust in a power greater than ourselves. Our happiness and peace of mind depends on the degree to which we are willing to trust our God.

Complete trust in our God for the rest of our lives can be an overwhelming thought, but anyone should be able to accomplish it just for today.

My prayer for today is to place my complete trust in my Higher Power's will for me, knowing that whatever happens will be for my overall good.

E.J.K.
Moorestown, NJ

I try to think of my team members not just as "people I work with," but as *partners*. For they are partners. Partners we rely on to help us handle difficult situations. Partners who share the burdens of work, the responsibility of caring for others, the sorrows of failure. They are partners in the joy, too. They are there for me, to exchange favors. To confide in. To learn from. To teach. To just "be there" when I need a shoulder to cry on or a cheerful word to help me get going again. Today, I'm thankful for my fellow team members.

Anonymous

The ideal condition would be, I admit, that men should be right by instinct; but since we are all likely to go astray, the reasonable thing is to learn from those who can teach.

Sophocles

Wouldn't it be wonderful to be born all-knowing? Sadly, we are not. From the very beginning, we must go through the *process* of learning. At first, trial and error: we stand up, we fall, we try again. Next we learn from education, hard work, and experience. And the learning process never stops. We have opportunities to learn every day: seminars, meetings, workshops—all offering us the chance to expand our knowledge and improve our skills. Today, help me recognize an opportunity to learn all I can in this business of counseling. Grant me the self-discipline to take advantage of those opportunities.

Anonymous

I wish to tolerate your differences, and I hope you'll be gentle with mine. The Cherokee prayer asking that I not judge you until I have "walked the trail of life in your moccasins" touches my heart. I need this simple reminder to help me keep my life and work in balance and proportioned.

Sometimes I complicate my life by thinking too much. Today I want to keep my life simple and as nonjudgmental as possible. I experience my greatest feelings of freedom when I am able to recognize my likeness and connection to other human beings. Today, help me to let go of judgments and practice tolerance, to "walk in the moccasins" of every client.

S.C.
Dowagiac, MI

There are "musts" in each of my days in order to stay healthy:

Complete surrender to my Higher Power
Enough sleep
Prayer and meditation
Moderate, healthy meals
Vitamins
Twelve Step study and meetings
Reading a chapter of work-related material
Reading a chapter of recreational material
Meeting with friends for fun and support

I am grateful for my fulfilling, productive life and work. Help me to remember today that, as a counselor, discipline is the foundation of a healthy and happy life.

J.F.
El Camino, CA

To help others, I must be as aware of my own problems as I am of theirs. When I let my own troubles overwhelm me, I'm not helping myself or anyone else. Help me to find my way past false pride, to recognize when I'm in danger of becoming overstressed. Help me ask for assistance when I need it. And help me to be humble enough to accept it gratefully when it is offered. Today, I ask for the wisdom to know that I need help sometimes. My clients depend on me. Help me remember that asking for help is a sign of strength, not of weakness.

Anonymous

Today I take on a new family. It will be their first visit.

Help me to remember how it must feel for them to come inside a treatment center for the first time. The pain is raw and their understanding is still new. They are much more anxious than I am. How this anxiety may present itself is still unknown to me.

Let me make a special effort to remain relaxed and open to the newcomers. Help me be gentle with them, so their experience will be positive. If there are outbursts, help me remember that so much of the counseling experience is new to them. Whatever I can do to help these new clients, let me do it today.

J.S.
Crystal Lake, IL

None knows the weight of another's burden.

George Herbert

Today, I need help recognizing the pain of clients who seem "OK." So many shout their feelings that I may overlook the quiet ones, the eager helpers, the easy ones. Help me to remember that, beneath the surface, they carry the same pain of addiction. They, too, are struggling with self-hatred and denial and compulsion. Help me to remember that looks are deceptive. A smooth brow may hide a tortured soul. The client who fades into the background may be thinking about suicide. The over-eager "helper" may be practicing a form of denial. Today, help me give attention to each client in my care, not just those who shout the loudest.

Anonymous

"We shall overcome."

What wonderful inspiration for all of us, especially counselors working with addicted clients. Dr. King brought us a world of hope in three little words. To work in this field, we must believe that "we shall overcome." Overcome prejudice. Hatred. Addiction. Death. Fear. Insanity. Resentment. We shall overcome the waste of precious lives. We shall overcome the destruction of families. And find serenity. Productivity. Harmony. Love. Mercy. Joy. Peace. Today, these words will inspire my efforts. Today, as I work to help my clients recover, I believe that "we shall overcome."

Anonymous

(Here readers are invited to write their own meditation and make it part of the book. These opportunities
are placed on the 15th and the last day of each month.)

> *"God so loved the world that he didn't send a committee."*

This quotation is on a sign hanging behind a co-worker's desk. I like these little "nudges" and reminders in my day that help keep things light. I have a sign on my desk that says,

> Rule #1: Don't sweat the small stuff.
> Rule #2: It's all small stuff.

I sometimes lose my sense of perspective and humor. When that happens, the person in my chair becomes a burden to myself (and, I suspect, to my client as well). I'm so grateful for my sense of humor. It's spared me in the most difficult counseling situations over the years. I cherish this part of me and delight in finding laughing soulmates. Let me share my laughter today.

S.C.
Dowagiac, MI

*To love another person
Is to see the face of God.*

Victor Hugo, "Les Miserables"

We experience God through other people. He comes to us in the caring ways we see them. They wish for us only what is best for us, and they help us grow.

Have I let people experience God through their love for me? Have I suppressed my feelings, my good qualities? Today, help me to love another unconditionally; only then can I know God.

*B.G.
Moorestown, NJ*

If I stopped counseling today, the counseling profession would progress without me, and after some grief, my clients would, too.

Sometimes I get my days and weeks out of balance. I find myself hurrying and rushing as if I were the missing piece in people's puzzles. When I am filled with self-importance, I become a burden to myself and others. I *am* of real value, and I do have much to contribute, but I need to remember that being a big cheese gets me nothing but mouse bites.

Today, help me to remember that I am not indispensable.

S.C.
Dowagiac, MI

I spend so much time thinking that sometimes I forget my mind is housed in a physical structure with its own special needs. My mind and spirit are important to my life, but my body needs care, too.

The right food helps me look and feel my best. Regular exercise tones my muscles and rebuilds bones. For clear thinking and a serene disposition, I need plenty of rest. Regular checkups, medical and dental, help keep physical problems to a minimum. Relaxation techniques help keep my heart and circulatory system strong.

My mind won't work properly if I ignore my physical being. To be at my best, for myself and for my clients, my body must get the attention it deserves. Let me remember to take some time for my body today.

Anonymous

The measure of a person is not whether we fail—we all fail at something, some time—but rather what we do with failure. Will we let failure defeat us? Fill us with self-pity? Will we give up and spend our lives blaming fate, or the heavens, or others?

Or will we accept the challenge, pick ourselves up, and start over again, resolved to work harder at succeeding?

When a client relapses, it's easy to be discouraged, to "give up" trying to help. We may think about changing professions, looking for something easier. But if we look around, we'll see so many who are recovering, who keep working at it every day. They didn't give up—maybe they had a counselor who didn't give up, either.

I have not failed when a client relapses—I have failed when I quit trying to help. I ask for help to persevere today.

K.I.
Chicago, IL

I'm tired today, and I need help controlling my temper. Help me to remember that, to the clients at our center, I am a role model, a walking advertisement for sobriety. Help me to realize the impression I make on others, even when sharing a joke in the hallway. Help me to hold my tongue, no matter how exasperated I get. Help me to be aware of how I look, how I sound, and how others see me. Help me to remember that, like it or not, clients view me and my team members as examples of sober life. Although I feel like throwing a tantrum today, please help me to present a dignified image to those around me. Help me to vent my negative feelings away from those who look up to me. As counselors and as people, we are always learning from each other. Today, help me inspire by my example.

Anonymous

I wake to the joy of a brand new day.

Eagerly I go forth, knowing I will be guided by my Higher Power in thoughts, actions, and ideas, as I work with others to discover their true selves. I think through my schedule, confident that our work together will be of benefit.

Help me to be a more effective channel that I might share my health, love, and serenity with all I come into contact with today.

Today is going to be a wonderful day. With all the promise of a new day, I know something good will happen for me and my clients.

C.C.
Katy, TX

Working as an alcoholism/substance abuse counselor, January usually means long hours and a heavier-than-usual caseload. That's because many people wait until "after the holidays" to come into treatment. And if they *can* wait that long it may mean that their chemical dependency has not yet progressed to the late stage . . . a good sign.

They are ready to work, and so am I. Their work is to tell me their secrets, especially the secrets that relate to their chemical use. *My* work is to *help* them to tell me their secrets. I'm not sure who works harder. They whisper, moan, plead, shout, cry, lie, deny, try. I listen, plead, whisper, shout, cajole, teach, cry, try. Slowly . . . together . . . the work gets done. Today, help me remember that each thing happens in its own good time.

J.E.
Park Ridge, IL

Some clients seem to stay in a revolving door that moves in and out of recovery. It's been painful for me to watch a client relapse again and again. As a "good counselor" I used to send all varieties of "life boats and helicopters" to help a client out of that revolving door, trying to give them something to cling to. I had to get tired of throwing life preservers in order to step back and let go. I remember watching a wise alcoholism counselor sit straight up in her chair during a difficult staffing and pound a fist on the desk as she loudly proclaimed:

"Remember, God hasn't quit His job!"

There is always a "miracle" waiting to happen in recovery, but not usually on my timetable. It helps to remember the story of the man who detoxed 3 times and stayed sober on the 4th.

Help me remember to plan plans, not outcomes.

S.C.
Dowagiac, MI

Ironically, the more I help new team members feel welcome, assist another without being asked, and am clear as to what my obligations are to each member, the more I recognize my own humanity, my own talents, and the more remote elements in my nature.

I need my fellow counselors. Each individual is in my life for a reason. Through working with them as a group, it's uncanny how much I discover of my ever-emerging self, and how together we improve our professional abilities today. I am very grateful to them. Today, let me show it.

K.L.
Park Ridge, IL

Fatigue is an enemy of concentration. Being an effective counselor requires me to be as "present" as possible with my clients. There have been days when I've gotten off of my schedule and felt drained and tired. When I feel that way, my internal bells ring and self-care becomes a priority. I go home, leave the dishes, unplug the phone, and sleep 10 refreshing hours. There's another type of fatigue that doesn't respond to a night of "catch-up sleep." Burnout weariness is a depletion of energy and zest that feels bone-deep. This kind of internal exhaustion needs an immediate response. We counselors are challenged to practice what we preach to others when the going gets tough.

All of my days are gifts and I deserve to live with all my health and energy available. When I'm down in the dumps, I need the best physical and emotional support available to regain my balance. Today, let my own well-being be one of my priorities.

S.C.
Dowagiac, MI

The need for acceptance does not end with growing up. Hanging in our kitchen window, with the sun shining through, is a gift from a friend. On its stained glass is an Arabian Proverb:

"Oh, the comfort—the inexpressible comfort of feeling safe with a person—Having neither to weigh thought nor measure words, but pouring them out just as they are—chaff and grain together—certain that a faithful hand will take and shift them—keep what is worth keeping and with a breath of kindness—blow the rest away."

These are a few of the gifts that help us grow one day at a time: Faith in our Higher Power. Love from our friends. Acceptance of ourselves. Pride in our work. A "thank you" from a client. I pray for the vision to see what is worth keeping today.

M.&D.E.
Denton, TX

Wear your learning, like your watch, in a private pocket; and do not pull it out and strike it, merely to show that you have one.

Earl of Chesterfield

Fresh out of graduate school, I came bustling into the treatment center, throwing around 18-letter words and complicated phrases I'd picked up in class. One morning I was called aside by Barbara, a superb counselor on my shift. "Sam came to me today, and he asked to be assigned to someone else," she said. "He likes you, but he feels dumb around you." That was the end of Ms. Know-It-All. Now, before I meet with a client, I spend a quiet moment remembering those early days, when I thought I tried to impress others but only scared them away. Today, as I counsel others, help me remember to Keep It Simple.

Anonymous

Maturity impels the growing person to improve his mind, expand his knowledge and awareness, better himself in order to have a happier life.

As a counselor, I can only give what I have, and I can only give comfortably and confidently if I acknowledge the source of whatever I have. Perhaps a more difficult challenge is gaining a knowledge of my Higher Power's will for me. One thing is always certain, though. When I'm with a patient, it's my Higher Power's will for me to be there with that patient. At that precise moment, the power is available to me and I pray that I will be open to it and use it well to help others.

J.B.
Pinellas Park, FL

My favorite co-worker left yesterday for another job, and I have a blizzard of feelings about it.
Most of all, I'll miss her. She was a wonderful counselor, who taught me so much. And she was a good
friend, too. I've lost those quiet talks, that shoulder
to cry on. I'm a little jealous, too, because she's
moved on and I'm still here. I don't like that feeling, but it keeps coming back. I'm nervous and resentful, even a little angry, about the new person
who I'll meet for the first time today. Will we like
each other? Will we be able to work together? So
many feelings, so many questions, so much uncertainty. As a counselor, I know I must work through
these feelings and get past them. Today, I'll work on
letting go of my sadness.

Anonymous

The journey from one heart to another is never too long.

Two counselors in the Kingdom of *Recovery* were blindfolded and seated in the courtyard. King *Serenity* wished to find the wisest one to help his troubled son. Three subjects sat facing the counselors; they represented Anger, Envy, and Shame. The counselors were given five minutes with blindfolds off to identify each subject's emotions.

The first looked and said: "This is anger, see his red face and rageful look. This is shame, with his downcast head and eyes. And this is envy; his glance is covetous." "Excellent," cried the King.

The second counselor asked each one: "How do you feel?" Anger replied, "I am full of hurt." Envy sobbed, "I am consumed with fear of my inadequacy." And Shame whispered, "I feel worthless."

Good King *Serenity* appointed the second counselor to the royal court. "One is truly wise who knows that only by viewing the heart can a person be truly seen."

I pray for the widsom to listen to another's heart today.

S.C.
Dowagiac, MI

Without FAITH
    Can there be trust and caring?

Without HOPE
    Can there be dreams of accomplishment?

Without FORGIVENESS
    Can there be promise for the future?

Without LOVE
    Can there be tolerance, acceptance, beauty,
        and growth?

Today I pray for the wisdom to see one
instance of each of these qualities.

F.A.
Chicago, IL

Every age can be joyous.

Childhood is simplicity and energy, innocence and curiosity. Running, laughing, weeping, learning, children express all their feelings and endlessly explore their universe.

Young adulthood brings emerging power. Character is cemented, beliefs refined, finding a place in the world. This is a time of most serious study, learning what we must, to become who we want to be.

Middle age has softer pleasures. Serenity is our power, and we smile gently at the tumult of the young.

Old age brings wisdom and peace. Shorter lives value each day; our eyes are newly opened to the beauties of the world; moments appear in crystal clarity.

Today, let me be grateful for the pleasures of my age. And let me appreciate clients and co-workers of every age.

Anonymous

But how shall we expect charity toward others,
when we are uncharitable to ourselves?
Charity begins at home.

Sir Thomas Browne

If my basket is filled with plums
    I can't give you apples
If my heart is filled with self-hatred
    I can't teach you self-love
If I can't forgive myself
    I can't grant you forgiveness
If I'm obsessed with perfection
    I can't teach you tolerance
If my body trembles with anger
    I can't teach you serenity
If I can't love myself
    I can't love you

Let me remember today that, especially as a
counselor, charity begins at home.

Anonymous

"Happiness is found along the way, not at the end of the road."

Most of my life, I wanted to hurry to accomplish something, achieve success, be somebody, so I could "be happy." I hear others saying this, too: "Just five more years at this job, then I can retire and be happy." Or, "If I could just stop drinking or using drugs, I could be happy." It's a trap that's easy to fall into, viewing our day-to-day life as something to be endured until we can improve, achieve, or succeed— and "be happy."

Then one day I saw a sign that said, "Happiness is found along the way, not at the end of the road." Reading it, I began to better understand the concept of "One Day At A Time." It seemed I was always struggling for tomorrow, never thinking about "today" until it became "yesterday" and a memory. I was only living tomorrow and yesterday . . . missing today altogether. Let me remember as I start my day that serenity is in today. The work I do today, the people I meet and see, are "just for today."

N.H.
Muscle Shoals, AL

Caregiving vs. Caretaking

Being a professional helper is a gift. How I use the gift is important. Do I use it in the true sense of helping others help themselves? Or do I sometimes use it to help myself hide? Do I get lost in others' lives in order to bury my feelings or gain a sense of my own worth?

I need to grow; to grow, I need to experience and accept my feelings as they are. I can do that through being a caregiver versus a caretaker. Giving begins with me. I can't give care to others if I give little or no care to myself.

Today, help me practice giving and doing for myself what I would truly give and do for those I care for. Help me realize that my self-worth comes from within, and is about who I am, not what I can do for others.

A.S.
Denton, TX

Early in my career, I felt responsible for clients who relapsed. I spent hours torturing myself, wondering what I'd done wrong, what would have stopped him or her from relapsing. I couldn't let go. I felt responsible for so much—what a burden I made myself carry!

Now I know that recovery and relapse come from joint effort of the client, his or her Higher Power, the treatment team, and many other factors. The burden is not mine to bear alone. My responsibility is being the best counselor I can be, period. No more, no less.

Now, when I "lose" a client, I know I did my best to help. Today, I ask for the humility to accept my essential, but limited, role in a client's success or failure, and to let go gracefully.

Anonymous

True forgiveness requires true forgetfulness.

Do I know someone who doesn't "deserve" to be forgiven? What a heavy burden, to carry pain and hurt from the past. Practicing the gentle art of forgiveness seems very important to me today. My energies and gifts are not as available when I am unwilling to forgive. My insides begin to feel like a river whose flowing channels are blocked, and I lose sight of the beauty in you and me.

Sometimes it feels like a sacrifice to "give up" my past injuries. Sometimes I've nursed them so long, they feel like a part of me. Would I have an empty hole inside if I let go? Will I need to do some grief work first?

God forgives—do I know something that He doesn't? Is there someone I haven't been willing to forgive?

I pray for the strength to begin by forgiving myself.

S.C.
Dowagiac, MI

A friend stays when others walk out
A friend lends a hand when others fold theirs

A friend sees with loving eyes
A friend listens with loving ears

A friend takes time to know you
A friend lets you know her

A friend needs holding close
And a friend needs freedom

A friend loves you
For what you love in yourself

Today, let me love my friends
And let my friends love me.

S.B.-P.
Houston, TX

Help me to remember that the rules I use to counsel others must apply to me, too.

I can't ask a client to be honest if I'm hedging on the truth. I can't expect him to learn self-discipline if I show up late for a session. I can't demand she pay attention to me if my mind is elsewhere. I can't expect sensitivity from him if I'm abrupt and thoughtless.

Help me to think before I act, to realize the consequences of my behavior and the lessons others learn from me, even when I don't realize I'm teaching. Only when my own life is in order, can I expect the same from others.

Today, help me to practice what I preach.

Anonymous

Gratitude is my capacity to gladly welcome and appreciate the unique achievements, difficulties, and voids of each day.

Life's timing is seldom predictable. Blessings abound in areas without my slightest effort, and problems appear in the least expected corners. When joy and struggle come my way, I rarely feel spontaneously thankful. It's *my* role to find gratitude.

Using my abilities for productive work, love, and thought is one route to that appreciation. My sense of meaning and contribution is strengthened when I use my energies to serve others, or just to be present at their critical life moments.

Paradoxically, when I invite what awaits me, even disappointment and regret underscore my need for intimacy with others.

Today, my preventive medicine of the spirit is like physical exercise that detours disease and stiffness. Just as stretching limbers my body, exercising my sense of gratitude will allow me, like nature, to have the capacity for renewal.

May I catalogue now those people and events I'm grateful for today, and in so doing, invite serenity.

K.L.
Park Ridge, IL

Wanting to be something can mark the beginning of growth, but intentions alone are never
enough. Sighing for success won't get me anywhere.
Longing to help clients is useless if I don't put my
feelings into action. Wanting to be loved is doomed
if I don't seek to be a loving person. Dreaming of an
education leaves me ignorant if I don't pursue learning. In every area of life, intentions without action
come to nothing, help no one, produce nothing. Action helps me feel in control of my life; inaction
makes me feel empty and hollow and fosters self-
pity. Today, let me think about what I want, and
then act to make my vision a reality. Help me take
the necessary steps to foster my professional devel-
opment.

Anonymous

Peace is my internal blessing. When things are hectic, I always crave to have peace return. I think "crave" is a good word to use in talking about my increasing need for peace and serenity. My personal road to peaceful times has been long and filled with less-healthy cravings that blocked my flow of peace and contentment. But over the years, my life has become increasingly healthy and more meaningful and I have begun to experience a "peace of conscience" that I crave to experience again and again. This peace enhances and expands my life as a counselor and friend to myself and others. When I feel off balance, I look to my spiritual life for a solution. Then, my balance and sense of perspective return, and peace and rightness follow.

I was struck by the words of a spiritual director I met on a retreat. In talking about his personal relationship with God, he said, "I crave time with Him." Today, I crave time with Him, too.

S.C.
Dowagiac, MI

Today is for lovers, and I want to be one. Not just of one person, that's not enough—today, I want to be a lover of all humankind. To look at the great, bustling world around me and see the goodness there. I want to relish the differences in my clients, the variety that lives in each of us, the secrets of the soul and the heart, the joy and pain that set us apart from one another—yet bind us so tightly.

Today, I want to love others as I'd like to be loved myself, warts and all. Today, no matter the provocation, I won't think an unloving or unkind thought. I'll refuse to be drawn into the petty meanness of office gossip or the misery of the newspaper.

Let this be a step on my road to serenity. Today, I will be a lover.

Anonymous

Gifts, gifts, gifts—how we love them! But only if they come as gifts, not as deceits. Only if they express goodness, and are not presented as bribes. If they are acts of thoughtfulness, with no strings attached.

When we have a message, we can say it with a gift, and it will keep speaking for us. For the giver himself with every gift.

Let me remember all that a gift is, and let me give of myself with all my gifts.

S.B.-P.
Houston, TX

As an Adult Child of an Alcoholic, I used to pray only for relief from pain and fear. Now, I pray out of gratitude for the many insights my childhood gave me. You see, I must work especially hard to see others as they really are, and not as an extension of my dysfunctional family of origin. That extra work has an unexpected benefit: by examining others more closely, I may see each client more clearly. As a counselor, this extra effort helps me to develop rapport. The pain of my early life helps me relate to clients in their terms. I'm grateful now for what used to be a "disadvantage."

How wonderful that my pain has turned to compassion! Today, I'm thankful to be me. And I gratefully pray for continued growth.

Anonymous

No one is responsible for my problems and solutions but me. That's a depressing thought!

But with help from my Higher Power, I can be responsible for my problems, and for my successes, too. That's better. I have all the choices at my fingertips. If I don't like my job, I can change my feelings, or I can get a different job. If my friends don't understand me, I can help them to understand, or I can find different friends. If I'm feeling lonely or sad, I can take steps to change my mood. Everything I touch is mine to change.

Today, I'll take responsibility for all of my life, the bad and the good, and all the choices I make.

Anonymous

The Child is father of the man
And I could wish my days to be
Bound each to each by natural piety.

William Wordsworth

I think if a person will be God, he or she becomes even less a person. I grew up believing I should never admit defeat, always try to win, gain control and power over any situation, get to the top, and never give up. After several years as an alcoholism counselor, I see things differently. Now, I believe the more I seek control, the more control I lose. The more I strive for power, the more I become a slave to the illusion of control.

Real surrender lets me be "the child who is father of the man." It opens to me the reality that all life, and therefore all recovery, begins with full acceptance of healthy dependency, helplessness, unmanageability, and powerlessness. Let me accept myself today.

J.B.
Pinellas Park, FL

Today, I will remember that, alone, I do not have the power to start someone on the road to recovery. But working in a partnership with my Higher Power, my team members, and the person I desire to help, I can *facilitate* the process. When I become frustrated with one who refuses to follow my suggestions or to follow the Steps, I must remember that I'm in control only of myself. I will not allow myself to confuse powerlessness with a lack of skill. I will not let another's unwillingness to work a program interfere with my own. I can help others only when I follow my own rules. Today, help me keep foremost the fact that I am simply a tool that, when used, works to build the foundation for sobriety.

P.R.
Katy, TX

Defer not 'til tomorrow to be wise,
Tomorrow's sun to thee may never rise.

William Congreve

If today were not the first day of our lives,
but the last—how would we spend it? I'd gather my
loved ones around me and tell them, some for the
first time, how I feel. I'd pour out my heart and soul
to them, so they would know how I loved them before it was too late. I'd give them possessions I want
them to have, something to look at that reminds
them of me. I'd touch their hair and faces with my
hands. I'd look at each long and deep, seeing clearly
their unique beauty. Let me live each day as if it
were the first—*and* the last. Today, I won't let the
sun set on unspoken words of love.

Anonymous

In the days when "Easy to be Hard" from the musical "Hair" was written, there were causes to be fought and protests to be marched. But, as the song said, it is easy to be hard on those close to us, even while we're busy helping everyone else.

In the everyday rush of group, one-to-one sessions, meetings, and paperwork, it's easy to be hard on our fellow team members and ourselves. In our commitment to meet the needs of the people we serve, it's easy to forget our own needs for understanding, affirmation, respect, and caring.

Even when we're fighting for the cause of recovery in the larger society outside the facility, it's easy to be hard. Mistrust and criticism flow easily between physician and counselor, recovering and non-recovering people, insurance payers and treatment providers—anyone who doesn't see addiction and recovery just as we do.

Today, I will be a little softer on my team members and myself, "who should know better;" on professionals, "who don't understand the disease;" and on administrators, "who only worry about money."

D.M.-L.
Marblehead, MA

Many of the people I counsel are married. Sometimes the spouse is addicted, sometimes not. Always, there is emotional distance between husband and wife. There are many needs unmet, and many issues that are totally unresolved.

My job is not to decide whether two people should be married. My job is to listen to them and counsel them toward making their own decisions. Often their real pain is obscured by anger and resentment. Thanks to my training and abilities, I can see that.

I will go slowly with my married clients today.

Anonymous

An attitude of helpful expectancy can serve me very well today. My Higher Power has my day in His hands. Whatever happens, it will go most smoothly, and I will feel best about myself, if I am open to what the day brings, and at peace with whatever it holds for me.

I can give my best if I do not get bogged down in hurt, anger, and resentment. Instead, I'll try to trust in my Higher Power. I'll have faith that good will come my way. Help me today to be flexible and willing in my work with clients. Help me to learn trust in a new way.

B.R.
Park Ridge, IL

Many times I have pondered the challenge of the Serenity Prayer in my life, today and when I was first introduced to recovery. At first I prayed for serenity, quiet from my spinning thoughts and turbulent feelings. Next, acceptance for things that seemed unchangeable. I'd been over-responsible for years; to find out it was not my fault or responsibility was both frightening and a great relief. Finally, I was told I must have the courage to change the things I could. What were those things? God had given me intelligence and strength of will and many tools to work with; I knew my life could change dramatically for the better if I had the courage to face myself. The acceptance and unconditional love I received helped me learn the difference between what was to be changed by me, which was me—and what was to be accepted, which seemed to be almost everything else.

Today I know my primary job as a counselor is my *own* program of growth. As I change and grow, *everyone in my life* will change, too. There is never-ending renewal if I listen to the simple message of the Serenity Prayer.

M.E.L.
Denton, TX

There's an old saying that the optimist sees a glass as half-full, the pessimist sees it as half-empty. Every day, things happen, good and bad. We all enjoy the good things. But the bad, the negative experiences, the hurt and sorrow—how we react to these show what we're really made of.

Out of misery, we can find serenity and growth—or we can see the glass as "half-empty," and become bitter and resentful. We can learn the lessons life has to teach us—or we can retreat into a shell of self-pity.

I will be presented with many situations that bring this choice into focus. Today, I pray for the humility and wisdom to see the glass as half-full.

Anonymous

"Turning it over" is a step-by-step, one-day-at-a-time process.

It is growing in two directions: getting to know our Higher Power, *as* we come to know and understand ourselves. We could compare it to the growth of a tree: The roots grow down into the soil for food, while the branches grow up into the light, turning the nutrients into new life. Like the tree, we grow spiritually by looking deep within ourselves, while we aspire upwards to conscious contact with our God.

As we draw from within the knowledge of who we really are—our assets and liabilities—we can explore these in light of our relationship with God and others.

This Higher Power who created us also cares for us. That is reason enough this day to maximize our assets and minimize our liabilities.

T.B.
Park Ridge, IL

I always want to be a dreamer, to feel a yearning inside to make my vision happen. When I dream, I feel connected with the best of me.

I've always been an "idea maker," but I had trouble making my dreams a reality. I started out excited and motivated, but would gradually slow down and find a reason to stop along the way.

A friend mentioned that many people have great ideas, but give up when the going gets tough. At that moment, I decided to change. I chose two half-finished projects and vowed to follow through, no matter what. That decision changed the path of my dreams: one project is finished, the other is underway.

Becoming more focused benefits my professional life, too. I think before making commitments, and follow up as soon as possible. Daily follow-through on the small tasks gives me the time and creativity for bigger projects.

Thanks, today, for my dreams.

S.C.
Dowagiac, MI

Nothing in the world lasts
Save eternal change.

Marquis de Ragan

Don't give up on a rainy day; the sun will shine
again

Don't give up on love; practice loving

Don't give up on a task; perseverence will help you
finish

Don't give up on a friend; he may be in pain

Don't give up on a client; she may recover
tomorrow

Don't give up on yourself; your potential has not
been reached

I pray for the strength to persist today.

Anonymous

Yesterday was a terrible day! We got a new client, and he's trouble with a capital "T." Hostile, arrogant, resistant to all our efforts to help him. Yesterday I wasn't prepared, and didn't do very well. But today will be different. Today, I'm going to remember that addiction is characterized by denial; that the more difficult a client is to work with, the more he needs our help. Today I don't want to let myself be turned away by negative behavior. I won't let my personal feelings come between me and any client. All our clients need my clear thinking today. Help me to remember that the eager-to-please may be complying, the quiet one may be a "lost child" who needs to be drawn out. Help me to recognize denial in all its forms, so I can help those who need help.

K.I.
Chicago, IL

I need to remember that my ability to counsel others is God's gift to me. Others are helped, but it must also be essentially my blessing. I am in a privileged position—to see a spark of hope, a breakthrough in denial, some real tough honesty.

Recovery. It is truly my blessing. Today, I ask to be worthy of my gift.

D.N.
Fox River Grove, IL

*One of the highest forms of healthy self-love
is demonstrated
in our self-disciplined
commitment to balance.*

"Physician, Heal Thyself." As a counselor, do I give myself the same good care and concern that I suggest for my clients? I have an old dear friend who was an alcoholism counselor for years. She often commented on how she struggled for balance in her own life. She finally came up with a simple formula that worked for her: to remain an effective, productive, happy counselor and human being, she needed to keep a working balance in her life. Regularly, she would do a balance check, asking herself: "Is more than *one* major area of my life in disruption?" She regularly did a spot-check inventory of the physical, social, family, work, financial, and spiritual areas of life. If she found a significant problem in more than one area, she made an immediate effort to re-establish more personal stability. Am I in need of a life balance check? Today, I will take time for my own spiritual health.

S.C.
Dowagiac, MI

Of all the negative emotions, resentment diminishes us the most. It brings unwarranted anger toward those who have something we want, and self-pity for ourselves. It drains us of the energy we need to change our lives and work toward goals. Resentment keeps us in a rigid judgment of who "should" and who "should not" achieve success; all "should" attitudes are pointless, breeding discontent and wasting time. Above all, resentment is ugly to see and even uglier to feel. When I'm resentful, I feel hatred toward others and myself.

Today, I ask for the humility to accept my limitations, without resenting others who have exceeded them. I ask for the courage to pursue my own goals, not comparing myself to others.

Anonymous

I ask patients daily to assess their relationships, but do I? I have a responsibility to each of my team members, a responsibility to help each one come closer and closer to their individual and group professional potential. Perhaps I provide a suggestion, an honest feedback comment of their performance, or just an "ear" about a difficult client situation.

Do I inspire my team and bring vitality to it? Or do I drain it of its much-needed team energy? Managing the inherent tension and joy in any close working group calls upon us all. Just like an athlete, the team's excitement, spirit, and common direction can overcome any grueling situations or obstacles. Today, I ask for the help to contribute to my team's vitality.

K.L.
Park Ridge, IL

This is a day that will be full of events; today I will take time for me. It often seems that there isn't enough time in a day to accomplish all I'd like to. Because I'm in a helping profession, a great deal of my day will be spent attending to the needs of others. But, if I spend my entire day giving to others and do not stop to replenish myself, I soon will have nothing to give.

I've been blessed with the gift of being able to help others. Help me give myself the support and guidance I need to make time for myself, as I continue to grow in learning healthy self-love. Today, I will set aside some time "just for me."

A.S.
Denton, TX

When someone acts unkindly, they are usually afraid.

There are some days when I wake up afraid. The cure that seems to work is to get two feet on the floor and start moving. Usually, my day gets brighter when I get moving and the butterflies in the pit of my stomach begin to fly in formation. Sometimes, I wonder why it's harder to love and accept the scared little child inside of me, than it is to accept my clients and their insecurities and fears. What wonderful days I have when I'm willing to love my best and not fear my worst.

Today I will give to myself the same gifts of acceptance that I give to my clients.

S.C.
Dowagiac, MI

I can never forget the pain I felt when my nephew commited suicide after years of struggling with his chemical dependency. He was 21 years old. Many of my patients at this time were also young. My family was of great comfort to me at this difficult time. My own son, who had 7 months of recovery, was especially consoling. He said, "Mom, no alcoholic dies in vain." I had heard these words several times before but discovered great peace after hearing this phrase from my son. It gave me the strength to continue my ministering, *one day at a time.*

Today, I learned my Higher Power works through families. What wonderful gratitude came to me through someone very special in my life.

M.T.
Park Ridge, IL

I teach my clients to forgive themselves
    Do I forgive myself?
I teach my clients to avoid perfectionism
    Do I avoid perfectionism?
I teach my clients to go to meetings
    Do I go to meetings?
I teach my clients patience
    Am I patient with myself?
I teach my clients self-discipline
    Do I have self-discipline?
I teach my clients to love themselves
    Do I love myself?
I teach my clients, "Let Go, Let God"
    Do I?

Today, let me practice what I teach.

K.I.
Chicago, IL

I am only one,

But still I am one.

I cannot do everything,

But still I can do something.

And because I cannot do everything,

I will not refuse to do the something that I can do.
Edward Everett Hale

Today I pray for the courage to ask for help.

What I think about surrounds me. What I allow to be entertained in my mind becomes a reality. If I think negatively, I will attract negativity in my life. On the other hand, if I concentrate on developing positive thoughts, I will attract positive people and events to my life. My potential will be increased. I cannot control what thoughts come into my mind, but I can control my perception and reaction to them.

I pray that I may be filled with positive thoughts today; I deserve the resulting rewards.

A.S.
Denton, TX

*Spring fills my heart with so much awe
that I fear it might burst.*

With each new spring I shed another layer of worldly distractions and get one season closer to the real insides of me. I'm continually amazed by all there is to learn about my world. I'm touched by simple pleasures that become more dear to me with the passing days. There are endless beautiful places to visit, libraries of books to read, flowers to water color, red birds to watch, and lovely human beings to meet.

Sometimes I fear I might die in my middle years from too much joy! Can it be possible that I'm supposed to live and "practice being happy?" I know I'm now reaping some of the benefits of my years of personal growth work. As a counselor, what *hope* this brings me for my clients, when their journey seems endlessly long.

Today, I pray these flowers of hope and beauty inside me will warm the lives of those I meet.

*S.C.
Dowagiac, MI*

Am I having fun? As I begin or end my day, let me take time to remember how important fun is in my life. For in each of us is a "little boy" or "little girl" that lives in our heart. As I do my work, the seriousness, problems, and needs of our clients begins to drain me of energy, spontaneity, and creativity. When I feel this drain, let me stop and take a moment with my "little boy or girl," and make a plan to have fun today. I can detach and gain perspective, then return to my helping and guiding role. At the end of the day, let me take time to complete my "fun plan," be it a walk, play ball, a movie, a visit with a friend, a game, listening to music, or a special treat. Because in having fun, I too am healed.

Let me never forget that having fun with that "little boy or girl" who lives in my heart replenishes me with the creativity, spontaneity, and purpose I need to help others.

G.J.
Katy, TX

How can I keep forgetting music? It's the end of a busy week, I'm rushed, I'm frantic, and I can't figure out why. Then I remember: I haven't listened to music for several days. No wonder I'm out of sorts. For me, music is The Great Escape. It transports me, frees me from care, lets me dance on the clouds. After an hour of music, I can get through anything. Strangely, though, when my life gets tense, when work becomes a chore, I seem to forget this magic carpet. Or maybe I don't forget, but enjoy a brief spell of self-important martyrdom, oh, poor me. But self-pity doesn't satisfy much, and not for very long. So I get out the music, and get back on track.

Today, I give thanks for all the things that lift me up, and ask to remember them when I need them.

Anonymous

"The responsibility of tolerance lies with those who have the wider vision."

George Eliot

When I counsel with a narrow vision, I limit the recovery capacity of my clients. Today, I want to embrace the responsibility of tolerance that is the price of a wide vision. I get stagnant when I view only the small picture. Only in being willing to "let go" and believe in a larger plan can I understand relapse in my clients. I pray never to take relapse personally, but instead to see it as a necessary step some clients will make on the journey of recovery. As a counselor, I don't direct the trip and plan the destination; I'm only privileged to participate as a lantern-carrier. And I may be asked to exit the path at any point along the route.

Some days when I'm feeling overly-responsible for another, I find it hard to remember that it's the privilege of every human being to experience their own pain. I feel especially sad when my client relapses, but today I'm grateful that I don't have to be in charge of the big picture.

S.C.
Dowagiac, MI

Take time to work, it is the price of success
Take time to think, it is the source of power
Take time to play, it is the secret of
      perpetual youth
Take time to read, it is the foundation of
      wisdom
Take time to be friendly, it is the road to
      happiness
Take time to dream, it is hitching your
      wagon to a star
Take time to love and be loved, it is the
      privilege of the Gods
Take time to look around, the day is too
      short to be selfish
Take time to laugh, it is the music of the
      soul.

(An Old Irish Proverb)

L.M.
Argyle, TX

When it comes to continuing education, I've learned to listen more carefully to my second thoughts than my first. My first thoughts are usually childish reactions to the idea of added work; it takes a little thought to respond like an adult. But, like any unpleasant task, I may kick and scream at the idea of continuing education, groaning and moaning that I'm tired, I don't have the time, any excuse that seems plausible—yet I always complete a course or seminar with a wonderful feeling of accomplishment. One reason is I've learned something valuable. More important, I feel good because I completed a task I didn't want to do. Now, I have new information about my profession, and my self-esteem is enhanced, too. Today, I'll try to be grateful for the opportunity education brings to my continuing growth.

Anonymous

Many years ago, I worked for a company that was very unhealthy. We were understaffed, underpaid, overworked, and underpraised. But I wanted to stick it out. I thought they needed me, that I could make a difference. I thought they wouldn't survive without me.

One day in family therapy, I realized that, like the family of an alcoholic or drug abuser, I wasn't helping, but was actually enabling a sick system. My 'sacrifice' helped keep the problem going. And I was getting sicker, too.

With the tools I'd used to help that family, I confronted my own feelings, my fear of change, my need to "save" the company. Then, it was easier to make the changes I needed in my life. I'm grateful that I learned this lesson early in my career. Now, each morning, I take a hard look at my life, and make the changes I need to continue growing.

Today, will I be part of a healthy or an unhealthy system?

C.L.
Champaign, IL

The first day of spring, the season of rebirth. Though the wind blows and the sky has a winter bluster, there's a hint of spring all around. Soon buds will pop on the trees, then leaves and bees and birds. Grass will clamber through the mud almost overnight, with a sprinking of dandelions to delight the eye and frustrate the gardener. The squirrels are coming out, a little squinty-eyed from the winter sleep, their ears still tufted with winter's white, to dig up buried treasure. I feel renewed, too. My step is quicker, my heart a little lighter today. And today, I have a special thought for my clients. Working together, with the help of our Higher Power and the energy of spring, we can help make this day a special one on the road to recovery.

Anonymous

I treated him; God cured him.

Ambroise Pare

This was written by a doctor of medicine, but it applies to us counselors, too. Surely, if I could "cure" someone, no client I worked with would ever relapse. So when I'm tired and depressed and wondering what it's all about, I think of this saying. I can carry the message, but in the end, only my client and his or her Higher Power can effect long-term recovery. My burden is shared! I'm grateful for this beautiful thought.

Anonymous

There are moments in our lives as counselors that are "holy places." These special places remind us of where God has touched us in a special way. Perhaps it's a heart-felt thank you from someone who's struggling with recovery. Maybe it's that special Christmas card that keeps coming, now for the third year, reminding you that you were their counselor. Or that breathless, halting greeting: "I've just come back to show you my first year coin."

These infrequent special moments, "holy places," often come at times when we seem the most frustrated and harbor the most doubts. Coming unexpectedly, these special events fill us with wonder.

These aren't the "holy places" where pilgrims venerate shrines of past miracles. Or are they? Our "holy places" are just as special, just as miraculous, for they are about the miracles of recovery. Today, may I look back to find comfort and strength, and remember with joy the "holy places" that are cherished in my heart.

S.G.
Denver, CO

Make each day count! Give yourself to every dawn of renewed hope. Look for love, forgiveness, tolerance, optimism, temperance, industry, faith, and righteousness. Don't squander this day on cynicism, hate, envy, faultfinding, pessimism, gossip, doubt, or anger. Let the days of life not add up to years, but to moments of joy and love and happiness. Don't my clients deserve this? Don't *I* deserve this?

Today, I will take time out to cherish my life.

S.B.-P.
Houston, TX

I need to remember that turning my will and life over to my Higher Power includes each moment of a counseling session. When I allow thoughts of "if only . . ." to haunt me, I've forgotten my contract with my Higher Power. I only frustrate myself when I give undue time to wishing I'd made a particular point, comparison, or pursued a certain avenue of thought. It's good for me to pray for guidance as often as possible in my day, then trust that I've said all I needed to say in a session—it was complete. I have no "magic words" to turn on lights in someone's head.

Today, I will trust that my Higher Power honors my commitment to my Third Step even, or especially, as I work. Timing is important. And my Higher Power's timing is perfect.

D.N.
Fox River Grove, IL

Things pile up sometimes. The needs of others seem so pressing that my own get lost. My clients are so important that I put off the seminar I should attend, the paperwork that needs to be finished. At times like this, I try to remember a slogan from one of the Twelve Step programs: "Do the Next Right Thing." How this simplifies my life! I don't have to do everything right now—just one thing.

Figuring out which *is* the next right thing can seem confusing, but then I consider my priorities. Sometimes the client must wait until the paperwork is done. Sometimes leisure waits until work is finished. And sometimes *everything* has to wait until I've taken a break and cleared my mind. Today, help me to get my priorities straight, to "Do the Next Right Thing."

Anonymous

It's good to measure our lives by a positive gauge, by triumphs, and lessons learned, and good deeds performed. But sometimes that just doesn't work. There are awful days (we've all had them) when nothing good happens, and trying to find some goodness just makes things worse. On days like that, I counsel my clients (and myself) to make a mental list of all the awful things that *could* have happened—but *didn't*. Things like:

> I didn't drink or use drugs today.
> I didn't break confidentiality today.
> I didn't hurt anyone today.
> I didn't compromise my integrity today.
> I didn't let down my team members today.
> I didn't put off an unpleasant task today.

When this day ends, I pray to have some positive events to recount. If not, I'll use my list of what didn't go wrong for comfort.

Anonymous

I've been promoted. Now I have three counselors reporting to me. The promotion was a bit of a surprise and I'm not sure of my feelings.

Some of my feelings are good ones. I'm glad for the growth opportunity. I'm confident that I'm qualified and experienced and well able to handle the additional work. The idea of supervising others has always appealed to me. I'm excited about helping develop other staff.

But, like anything new, it makes me a little afraid. I'll stay in close contact with my supervisor and facility director over the next months. I'll share the feelings that I have. I'll be open to guidance and suggestion. I'll listen carefully to my subordinates before making major decisions. And I will have confidence in my decisions once I make them.

Let today be a period of growth for me. Keep me open to new experiences and ideas. My professional training has prepared me well, and I am ready to grow.

Anonymous

A thing of beauty is a joy forever:
Its loveliness increases; it will never
Pass into nothingness; but still will keep
A bower quiet for us, and a sleep
Full of sweet dreams, and health, and quiet breathing.

John Keats

Today, let me find a thing of beauty to meditate on.

Anonymous

*Man never falls so low
that he can see nothing higher than himself.*

Theodore Parker

We all carry God in our hearts. He may be hidden. He may be denied. But He is there. He may have another name, but He glows in each of us. No one is beyond his reach. No one is truly alone. He may be hidden, even from oneself, but He is there. May I help a client discover a Higher Power today.

Anonymous

The more fully I live, the more I grow, the more able I am to help others.

Urging my clients to relax, eat, sleep, play, give, and take—these are things that seem so obviously important to their recovery. And if I feel a well-rounded life is good for them, so must it be for me. Do I really believe the things I so clearly see as helpful to clients? If so, I must take the challenge of living my own life the way I feel is right for others in their recovery. Help me do it today.

D.N.
Fox River Grove, IL

How do I feel when a family is leaving our treatment center or group? Do I wish they were staying? Have I enjoyed working with them? Am I glad to be rid of them? Is there something I wish I'd said, but didn't? Is there one more issue I'd like to raise with them?

I didn't realize I had so many feelings about this. It's a part of the counseling process that's still unclear to me. I know each family is different and some families will do better than others.

Help me to take a few minutes today to reflect on my feelings about a family's departure. The good times. The bad times. The times when progress was so fruitful. The pain of disillusionment.

When a family leaves, they're scared. But it's also scary for me. I have many feelings about a family leaving. Help me to be in touch with my feelings and, if needed, discuss them with another staff member.

Anonymous

*Well-trained silence hath more eloquence than
speech.*

Martin Farquahar Tupper

Help me today to be still. My client needs time to hear what's been said. Time to think over a new idea. Time to trust. Let me be patient and give that time. Help me hold back, to let ideas penetrate and be absorbed. Let me respect my client's own timetable that can't be rushed or forced. Help me to present my thoughts one at a time, and not overwhelm her with too much too soon. Help me to demonstrate, rather than tell. Help me to *be*, rather than preach. Help me today to be still.

K.I.
Chicago, IL

There is no feeling in a human heart which exists in that heart alone—which is not, in some form or degree, in every heart.

George MacDonald

We're so very different! You're short and I'm tall. Your hair is red; mine is dark. You say "thank you" and I say "gracias." We're so very different, I think. Yet I've seen you weep in sorrow. I've heard you shout in anger. You tremble in fear, blush in love. The words are different. The skin is different. But the feeling is the same. Don't let me forget this today. Help me to remember how alike we are, you and I, who are so different.

K.I.
Chicago, IL

Ideals are like stars;
you will not succeed in touching
them with your hands.
But like the seafaring man on the desert of waters,
you choose them as your guides,
and following them you will reach your destiny.

Carl Schurz

To be a counselor, we must have vision. Pessimism and despair often surround us; only ideals can guide us to growth and recovery. We must be able to see a better world for our clients, and ourselves, too. Armed with this vision, we can face this day, and all those that come, with confidence and serenity. Today, I will remember my vision of a better life for my clients. I have faith in a better life for myself.

Anonymous

Habit, n.: a shackle for the free

Ambrose Bierce

Some habits are positive and healthy and important to cultivate. Others are deadly; they strangle my creativity and create a barrier between me and the world.

Are habits tying me down? Is my counseling routine blinding me to what's around me? Am I reading charts with fresh eyes? Am I paying attention to my surroundings? Am I thinking and counseling based on the needs of my client and the situation—or am I operating on "automatic pilot?" This new day gives me a chance to make a fresh start, to break some of the habits and change some routines. They are a barrier between what I am, and what I could be. Today, help me cultivate a positive behavior.

Anonymous

Children are indeed gifts from God. As parents, it is our job to take care of children, nurture them, and attend to their needs, emotional as well as physical.

Many of the families I counsel include small children; I often find them difficult and frustrating to work with.

Today, I will make a special effort to reach out to the small children and touch them. I will try to understand them and listen to their pain, the pain that comes with addiction in the family.

J.S.
Crystal Lake, IL

*A crust eaten in peace is better than a banquet
partaken in anxiety.*

Aesop

Counselors face uncomfortable issues—large
and small—everyday.

There will be times of sadness over things we
can't control, but we don't solve these issues by being anxious or fearful. In this state we are out of control and unable to think.

When we relax from the anxious state, we
can connect with that part of ourselves that is able to
deal with all human affairs. Today, let me remember
to relax. Help me to relinquish control, trusting myself to do what's best for me and others.

*S.B.
Chicago, IL*

I'm heading for burnout and I need to take some time for myself; yesterday I worked too late, and resented it, feeling angry at "those clients" who "made me" stay late. I'm irritable lately, for no good reason. Help me to let go; I talk and think about my work constantly and have trouble delegating responsibility. I'm talking more than listening, especially at home. Others don't seem to understand or appreciate me.

Help me take a break before I'm broken. Today, I'll leave the building for a few minutes, get out, walk around, forget my responsibilities for awhile, maybe find something to laugh about. Help me turn my concentration inward, to my own feelings and my own needs.

Today, help me do everything I can to stop the burnout before the flames start.

Anonymous

We talk about wearing two hats: being a counselor in the alcoholism treatment field, and recovering from an addiction. I wear a third hat: I'm also an ACOA, an adult child of an alcoholic. Sometimes, that makes my work harder, because I have to fight "seeing" my family in my clients. But coming from that background makes my successes much more satisfying, too, because I don't help just one person, I can help an entire family. Whether a client recovers or not, everyone in his life has a chance to resolve their problems and become healthy again.

My own childhood scars can be healed, and I can help the children in my client's family toward a happier life. What great peace that gives me! And with the help of my own Twelve Step program, I'm rediscovering the child in myself. Today, I look forward to my work. Help me to be ready to help that family, and myself.

Anonymous

Lord, give me the guidance to know when to hold on, where to let go, and the grace to make the right decision with dignity.

Marathon runners learn the painfully important lesson of running their own race. Going out too fast too soon can be exhilarating, a natural high, a "sweet moment." It can also spell disaster when "they hit the wall"—muscles screaming, stomach retching, feet of lead. Sometimes tucking in to a passing group will offer the needed fellowship and distraction from the discomfort and loneliness of the miles. Sometimes feeling the fullness of discomfort in solitude is an opportunity to spend time with God.

To run a good marathon, to work a good recovery program, to live a good life, to be a good counselor, there will be times when we will surrender to our powerlessness and hold on to one another. There will be other times when we will let go, turning our lives over to the care of God as we understand Him.

Thank you, Lord, for all 26.2 miles of the marathon, for being with me in my exhilaration, boredom, pain, and satisfaction.

S.W.R.
Park Ridge, IL

Andy M., who I counseled in treatment, is dead. He relapsed a few weeks after leaving and now, six months later, has died of alcohol poisoning. I need help to sort out and work through these awful feelings. I'm furiously angry at him; how could he throw his life away? And I'm angry at myself, because I didn't "save" him. I'm filled with sorrow for his family, and with frustration that I couldn't do anything to avoid this tragedy.

Help me to understand and forgive Andy. Help me to forgive myself, to remember how hard I worked to help him recover from his disease. Help me remember the client's who are sober and free, thanks to our efforts and the grace of God.

Anonymous

They said laughter is good for the soul—it's certainly good for *mine*. Counseling is such an intense, serious field; every working day, we're involved in the life-and-death struggles of our clients.

In spite of that—maybe *because* of that—many of us have a highly developed sense of humor, a keen appreciation of the comic absurdities, the pitfalls and pratfalls of life.

Laughter is a way to unwind from the day. It soothes the mind, relaxes the soul, and brings us closer to others. Laughter affirms life and helps me find communion with my Higher Power.

From a counselor, "comic relief" *is* relief. Today, I'll give thanks for laughter. Help me to bring joy to the lives of others.

Anonymous

No act of kindness, no matter how small, is ever wasted.

Aesop

An ex-client told this story:

"I was at the point of relapse, but I dragged myself to a meeting, even though I expected no help. I took an elevator to get there and I stood in the back, feeling very low. A young woman got on, turned to me, and asked what cologne I was wearing; she wanted to get some for her boyfriend. I told her, she got off at the next floor, and went her way. But that was the turning point for me. I remembered my drinking years—no one smiled and told me I smelled good then. Such a small thing, but I suddenly felt great—and I realized that *this* feeling was worth fighting for. I smiled at the woman as she went down the hall, unaware that she'd helped me win the hardest battle of my life."

Let me remember this client today. As I make my own way "down the hall," help me remind myself that no act of kindness is ever wasted.

Anonymous

Everyone wants to have a friend; today I'll try to *be* one. Your needs will come first; I'll save mine for another day. Instead of planning what to say, I'll really listen to you. I'll think of a question to ask—and not anticipate your answer. It's hard for me to come out of hiding sometimes, but today I'll try to share myself with you. If you come out of hiding too, I'll be careful of your secret. Talking about my feelings can sometimes be hard, but today I'll take some risks, trusting you to be gentle with me. All through this day, I'll be in touch with how much you bring to my life. How lucky I am to have a friend like you. Help me, today, to be a friend.

K.I.
Chicago, IL

In the early morning I often contemplate the events of the unfolding day with anxiety and fear. Sometimes I'm anxious about my job—there's so much to do; can I get it all done? Or the thought of someone I'll be seeing upsets me; what will happen? Maybe it's an upcoming event that worries me; how will I handle it? Post-holiday blues can attack; was all the work worth it?

On days like this, I need to remember three things:

> . . . to do whatever I reasonably can to prepare for the day;

> . . . to put my day in God's hands, and ask for help with the specific worries that are surfacing;

> . . . then bring my attention back to the positive aspects of the present moment.

I can trust my Higher Power to help me today with the details of my life whenever I take time to ask.

B.R.
Park Ridge, IL

Today, I will write a list of ways that I like to have fun, and I'll do at least one of them.

1. Get tickets for the next circus that comes to town.
2. Have a good three-minute belly laugh with a friend.
3. Have a "do nothing" day, and refuse to feel guilty.
4. Swap old paperbacks for "new" old paperbacks.
5. Ask someone I'd like to know better out for coffee.
6. Have breakfast in bed.
7. Register to take an impractical class.
8. Hang prisms in a sunny window to make indoor rainbows.
9. Buy fresh flowers for my desk.
10. Walk barefoot in the grass.

What will you put on your list?

Please open my eyes to the small pleasures of my life today.

S.C.
Dowagiac, MI

Common sense is not so common.

Voltaire

A continuing problem I've had as a counselor is thinking so much, analyzing so much, that common sense gets lost. I've spent hours researching a problem, only to have someone else sum up the problem *and* the solution in a few simple words.

Today, as I prepare for my day, I ask for simplicity. Help me to "get out of my head" long enough to see, simply and clearly, what needs to be done. Help me to regard my clients as people, not as problems. Help me to regain the common touch, to analyze when necessary, but not lose sight of simple, elegant solutions. Today, in the complexity of counseling, I pray for simplicity.

Anonymous

Often I find myself telling clients who are disappointed in relationships, or feel rejection from loved ones, or deprived of caring from parents, that people can only give what they have to give. I need to remind them not to place unreal expectations on people who have their own limitations.

As a counselor, I can only give what I have, too. I must gladly accept my gifts and use them well. I must also accept my limitations and not pretend to give what I do not have. I must willingly be genuine. Today help me learn to love myself as I am.

J.B.
Pinellas Park, FL

I always want to be respectful of the "power" I have as a counselor. It's my ethical responsibility to use my skills in the holistic interest of each client. There's a thin line between a tough-love approach and what has been called "scratch and bleed therapy." I have a responsibility to evaluate and plan my responses according to treatment goals based on the individual needs of each client. Most clients value honest confrontation done in a loving, direct manner. Timing is the key in deciding when clients are ready to really hear confrontation. Recovery can depend on breaking *through* a client's denial system— but breaking *down* a client in the name of recovery can do more harm than good.

Have I thought out the ways I use confrontation? Do I examine my motives? Do I seek regular supervision? Today, I will be aware of my effects on others.

S.C.
Dowagiac, MI

"Here I am, Lord, use me!"

This is a powerful prayer that I was taught some years ago to say in the morning. Sometimes I forget to bring God to work with me, and those days are never quite as good. When I begin my day with prayer, I notice that events seem to "fall into place," and there is a balance and rhythm in the hours. I don't need to have all the answers. I feel satisfied and centered on days when I pray, and I'm more "available" to myself, clients, and coworkers. Why do I neglect prayer on some days? I'm like a ship without wind. I forget who I am and my ego can lead me in the wrong directions.

Today, I don't want to be in the driver's seat of my life. I know I'll forget to slow down at the stop signs. I will pray this morning and practice not having "all the answers" today.

S.C
Dowagiac, MI

It takes a wise man to recognize a wise man.

Xenophanes

Do I recognize wisdom? We're all learning constantly, from everything and everyone that touches us. But what are we learning? Who are our teachers? Are we learning laziness from an idler? Manipulation from a cynic? Or are we learning grace and goodness and maturity? We can't choose those we work with, or those we counsel. But we can choose what we will learn, and who we will learn it from. Today, let me be aware of the lessons around me, and let me take care to learn wisdom.

Anonymous

As a counselor, each day I participate with people in breaking the bondage of addiction, discovering new freedom in recovery. Often I'm active in that process, offering encouragement and support. Other times I stand by, quietly watching the birth of recovery.

But I'm not a casual observer, for I, too, have things that bind me. Do I tend to overwork my perfectionism and insecurity? Do I fear to ask for help? These bind me, block my own growth and spiritual potential.

As in recovery programs using the Twelve Steps, my own freedom comes in willingness to accept my "powerlessness." Being powerless is the key that unlocks the bondage, for when I know where my power comes from, nothing can keep me from experiencing freedom, from experiencing serenity. Today, let me be open to "power" in my life that enhances my spiritual growth.

S.G.
Denver, CO

Everyone to his own.
The bird is in the sky, the stone rests on the land,
In water lives the fish, my spirit in God's hand.

Angelus Silesius

Of all the things we try to pass on to our clients, belief and trust in our Higher Power may be the most important. Without the support of a Higher Power, we are flawed, very human beings trying to help equally flawed, equally human beings. Only someone greater than either of us can lift the burden, only a belief in something all-powerful provides enough comfort to sustain us during the long, hard process of recovery. My prayer for today is filled with gratitude, for my spirit is in the hands of my Higher Power.

Anonymous

*I am responsible for my outlook and attitudes
and I have the choice today
of magnifying positive or negative.*

Visualization is an effective attitude-enhancer
that I use in my professional life. I have to develop a
mental image of how I want to be seen in my work
environment, then visualize, meditating on the
person I want to be today. I close my eyes and see
myself walking tall with shoulders back, smiling, full
of energy and health. I visualize personal encoun-
ters, being friendly and responsive to other human
beings. I imagine the smiles of my co-workers; I feel
their positive energy and acceptance. I picture
myself as a comfortable, relaxed, and happy member
of my working team. I visualize myself as in exactly
the right place to learn, grow and be happy today. If
there is a co-worker I feel tense with, I see that
relationship as healed and full of light. I do this by
mentally blessing and forgiving that person and
focusing on their good qualities. I also remember
that difficult people are my "teachers." After this
visualization exercise, I pray that it will be so for
today.

S.C.
Dowagiac, MI

Am I forgetting about my own recovery? Am I substituting my involvement with treatment for my commitment to a personal program of recovery? Am I assuming that knowing about addiction is "almost as good" as working my own program? Am I confusing giving a lecture on honesty with sharing during a meeting? Is my immersion in treatment clouding my priorities?

A clear understanding and acceptance of the "two hat" issue will make me a more effective counselor and will allow my recovery to flourish.

Today, I'll remember my powerlessness, and humbly make a new commitment to my own recovery. I pray for acceptance, commitment and clarity of thought.

B.G.
Hialeah, FL

Counseling requires a lot of keeping my mouth shut and learning when not to interpret and give advice. Sometimes we counselors who tend to be "caretakers" find this especially difficult; we find ourselves wanting to "fix" and protect our clients from the necessary journey of working through their pain, joy, and powerlessness.

Do I truly trust the "process" in therapy? Do I sometimes find it hard to stop interpreting, to trust that change will happen along with the footwork? Do I try to predict and control the outcome? Am I aware of asking more "why" questions, than reflective "what" and "how" questions? Am I able to wait through silences? I pray for patience and trust today so God's will may be done.

S.C.
Dowagiac, MI

Deeds say more than words—what we do is what we are. Man becomes the story of his own deeds. They make the person—and they tell what kind of person they have made. My life will be measured tomorrow in the deeds I perform today. Let them be worthy of my best. Let my deeds be reflected in today's interactions with my families and clients.

S.B.-P.
Houston, TZ

When I was little, we gave May Baskets, simple little paper baskets, usually cone-shaped (the easiest for tiny hands), with a paper handle. We'd fill the baskets with jelly beans, sometimes a small toy. Sneaking carefully to a friend's house, we'd hang the basket over the doorknob, ring the bell, and run. Back at home, we delighted in imagining our friend's reaction to finding our gift. Even if asked, we'd never admit to being the giver; that would spoil it.

That was my first encounter with the power of giving anonymously, without any thought to what I'd receive.

I'm grown now, but there are still May Baskets to give—emotional and spiritual ones. A smile for a stranger, unexpected praise for a co-worker, a note tucked into a loved one's lunch; all of these can be May Baskets. Today, let me remember the simple pleasure of giving anonymously.

K.I.
Chicago, IL

It's hard having so many roles—wife, mother, daughter, neighbor, friend, church member, counselor. How do we separate one from another? I learned early in my counseling career the need to separate home and work. It was a lesson structured for me by my Higher Power—I know I could not have planned it as well. When my children were two and three, I unexpectedly got the opportunity to work as a temporary counselor in a town 30 miles away. The job was good for me in many ways, but the lesson I will always remember is the long drive. It gave me the time I needed to make the transition from mother to counselor, and from counselor back to mother as I unwound on the drive home. It is only as I look back that I recognize how lucky I am to have learned to separate my roles early in my career. What will I do today to keep my roles separate? I pray for help today so I may keep my balance.

C.L.
Champaign, IL

As a young counselor, I felt terrible when clients relapsed. I ached for them, bled for them, prayed for them.

Then I had a child, and I watched him learn to walk. He fell down a lot at first. Then he'd pick himself up and try again, over and over, until he took his first tottering steps by himself. As I watched, I realized that the learning was not in the trying, but in the *fall*.

The same is true of our clients. Most of them have made many attempts to recover, and failed, long before entering treatment. Some must fall again before they learn.

I still hurt for those who "don't make it." I fear they may die before they learn. But I let go, now. Today, I'll remember the little boy who fell so many times before he learned to walk. I'll let my clients fall, if they must, in their attempts to recover. I pray to be there when next they try. And I pray that it works.

K.I.
Chicago, IL

My friend moved to another state, and I never told her how much I care. I can write and declare my feelings now, but I'm sad that I didn't do it while she was there with me. I wanted to tell her, but put it off, feeling a little embarrassed. I was sure that, another day, I'd feel more comfortable. Now that "other day" is past, never to come again.

Let me learn from the sadness I feel now. Let me remember this: There is only one "now," and I must use it, *now*. Help me not to hold back my feelings from another friend, a family member, a co-worker. Help me to remember how temporary all of life can be, that I don't pass up a chance to love someone now.

Anonymous

Lord, help me remember that nothing is going to happen today that you and I together can't handle.

An Old Preacher's Greeting to Each New Day

How wonderful to have a "silent partner" watching over me today! I trust in my Higher Power and know He would never give me a bigger burden than I can handle. When things are going well, He inspires me to do better. When I feel discouraged, He is my peace and my comfort. With His help, I have all I need to make this day good. No matter how difficult my work may be, with His help, as the old preacher says, nothing will come my way that we can't handle together.

S.C.
Dowagiac, MI

Acceptance is such an important feeling to have. As tiny tots, the hand of a parent can be scolding or accepting. A friend gave us a picture a few years ago reflecting the positive side. It was very simple. The sculpture of a strong, gentle hand with a child tenderly leaning into its warm accepting form. These words from *Isaiah 49:15* were next to it:

*"See! I will not forget you.
I have carved you on the palm on my hand."*

I pray to practice acceptance today in my work.

*M.&D.E.
Denton, TX*

*"Behold, I have set before you an open door,
which no one is able to shut."*

Revelations 3:8

Some days, faith is all I have to hang on to.
There are days when getting up is an effort, and for
a few moments I want to cover my head and go back
to sleep. There are times when I can identify why
I'm feeling low and make plans to improve my situation. Harder times are those when I'm not able to
easily sort out my low spirits, and need to just keep
walking through my pain, putting one foot in front of
the other.

On these low days, something more than me
gets me up: a belief that in spite of how I feel now,
life will get better. I'm grateful for the small spark of
faith inside of me that keeps me moving from one
day into the other, sure in the knowledge that God
is at my side.

My clients have an internal flame that glows
within them, too. I pray I always remember that. I
am a privileged partner on their journey back to
light.

S.C.
Dowagiac, MI

The mind, in proportion as it is cut off from free communication with nature, with revelation, with God, with itself, loses its life, just as the body droops when debarred from the air and the cheering light from heaven.

William Ellery Channing

My mind is hungry today. It needs to be up-lifted with spirituality, challenged with thought, stimulated with ideas. It needs company and soli-tude, noise and quiet. It needs a good mystery and a quiet poem. Today, let me remember to feed my hungry mind as I feed by hungry body.

Anonymous

Spring fever's got me, and I feel like a kid again. When the weather is so fine, the outdoors calls. I want to roll around on the grass. Go fishing with a cane pole, and throw back all the fish. Climb a tree and listen to the leaves. Wade in the fast-moving stream so cold it numbs my toes. I want to roller skate on a sidewalk, even if it means a few falls. I want someone to hold a jonquil under my chin to see if I like butter. I want to put my ear to a railroad track and find out if a train is coming, and I want to wave to the conductor when it does. I want to make a big noise, holler out loud, without feeling silly. I want to find seeds in my pants-cuffs when I get home.

When spring fever hits, there's only one cure: I'll drive to the country, where no one else is, and act like a child to my soul's content. Another day I'll be grown up. Today is a day to rediscover childhood, and bring joy to my middle-aged soul.

Anonymous

I want to be a counselor who stands up for what I believe in, but without attacking others. Over the years, I've tried to think before I speak; that has helped me grow in my ability to share and be heard.

I have strong conviction and ideals about my profession. I am grateful to have learned that I give away my power and lose credibility when I emotionally overreact. Some days, it's harder than others to stay in professional balance. I need to wait and sort out my thoughts when I'm not sure where I stand on an issue. I'm especially grateful that I will now speak up and share my thoughts out loud—even when I'm the minority opinion.

I pray to continue to grow in ability to reason, risk, and learn from others.

S.C.
Dowagiac, MI

*Are we to mark this day with a white or a black
stone?*

Cervantes

This is my day, to do with what I please. I
can make it happy, or I can make it miserable. I can
even make it happily miserable, if I feel like indulging in self-pity. But it's my day, all mine, no one
else's. I can't affect how others will treat me, but I
can decide how I'll react to their treatment. I can't
make a client recover, but I can help him try. I can't
change what others do, but I can decide how I'll behave in response. I can't stop the rain—but I can
bring an umbrella. I can make today wonderful. Today—a white stone.

Anonymous

A gift lasts such a short time. But helping others find the goodness within themselves—that can sustain a soul for a lifetime.

We all have faults and weaknesses. But each of us has, too, a vast store of wealth locked inside, if only we can learn where to look. Kindness and gentleness, intelligence and common sense, energy, drive and ambition, seriousness and mirth, integrity and spirituality—these are there, too.

Help me teach my clients to find the good in themselves. Help me to find it in myself.

Anonymous

Have you ever noticed how the squeaky wheels always seem to get the grease? Often the loud and spectacular gets the attention, while the quiet and ordinary goes unnoticed. In our varied roles, we can be overwhelmed at home and work with "squeaky wheels" who monopolize our time and energy. A major challenge for most of us is realizing that the "squeaky wheels" are not always most important . . . just most noticeable. The people who deserve our time and attention are frequently silent, unable to be heard over the noise. Even God does not forcibly enter our lives, but quietly waits for an invitation.

The wisdom to discern the music of life from its squeaky noises is a gift, given to those who care for their spiritual health. Spiritual recovery allows us to listen to those in our life who deserve to be heard. Today, may I listen to God, who waits to show me a better day.

J.A.W.
Chicago, IL

Are teenagers the hardest people in the world to work with? Or does it just feel that way?

I am *not* looking forward to the Carson family today, with their two teenage boys. Sometimes I get exasperated because I feel these boys are totally out of control. Often I just want to give up in despair.

Being a teenager is difficult enough, but the pain of addiction and poor communication must make it doubly so for these young people. Help me remember this, and guide me toward sources of help and information that can help me better understand them.

Is there a staff member at our center who has more experience with teenagers? A book I can read? A seminar I can attend? Today I will seek out the help I need to better understand this age group.

Anonymous

Fear is something addicted people know well. We struggle with it constantly. Sometimes it helps to think of "FEAR" as Future Events Appearing Real. Fear may be an inability to stay in "today"—and today should be our only concern.

In order to change the pattern of fear, we first need to be aware of what we're doing. Ask others to point out to us when we're projecting, getting ahead of ourselves. That can be a first step in changing. Next, it's helpful to make a list of the ways we can solve a problem. Finally, when we've chosen a plan of action, put it to work. Using this system, I've found that fears can be reduced tremendously, and we stay in "today."

Help me to confront my fears one day at a time, and to change my patterns.

And help me to understand the role that fear has played in the life of my clients.

S.S.
Park Ridge, IL

One of my clients is like a turtle—tucked into a shell that seems impossible to break through. So today, before I leave for work, I'll think through the tools that might help me break through that shell.

During our session together, I'll silently ask: What are you saying? How are you saying it? What does your body language reveal? Are your gestures sending the same message as your words? If not, what might the real message be? What questions can I ask you that will reveal what's happening with you? What have I experienced that's similar, so I can relate to you better? Do you need feedback from me? Or silence? Do you need gentle support? Or confrontation? What can I give you that will help you move to the next step in recovery?

Today, I ask for help in remembering to ask the right questions, and in paying attention to the answers.

Anonymous

*Grace is of music . . . and the wind, invisible to
my eye.*
*Grace is of my heart and soul, my guardian, first
and last friend.*
Celebrator of my spirit.

*Grace is hard to understand when I demand to
touch and see.*
It is the answer in between . . . the lines . . .
*Intuition opens the door to readiness—sometimes
doesn't a special coincidence . . . happen at just
the right time?*

*When I am utterly exhausted
Grace keeps me in the game.*

*We say that we don't deserve grace, or need any
special favors.*
*Why is it so hard for us to accept a gift we didn't
"earn"?*
That is EXACTLY WHY we are given Grace.
*Because we believe that we aren't "good" . . .
enough.*

Grace is my Higher Power's visibly invisible
proof of love, protection, and knowledge that we are
loved by God.

S.C.
Dowagiac, MI

As an infant matures, he or she recognizes who best cares for him. On the basis of this recognition and what he's experiencing, he gives himself to this caring person.

As a counselor my patients need me in a sense, but I also need them. The care of my will which can "run riot," and the care of my life which can get "unmanageable," depends on my good decisions to respond to the genuine love and concern that exists in positive interpersonal relationships. I need to view it as God's presence and rely on its efficacy.

Today, I will make a decision to turn my counseling over to the care of my Higher Power, who will always help me accept my patient where he is, as opposed to demanding him to be where I want him to be.

J.B.
Pinellas Park, FL

Time was, I was a "night person." I dragged myself out of bed at the last possible moment, then rushed to work, arriving mussed and harrassed, exhausted before the day even started. Then a client told me his reason for early rising: "Because there's more life then." Those words struck my imagination, and I decided to find out what he meant first-hand. It wasn't easy to make such a big change in my life, but gradually I, too, became a "morning person."

Now, I'm often up to greet the dawn. The air is cool and a little damp. The view from my window is of stillness and peace; even the birds are quiet. They ruffle their feathers, preen and fluff and seem to stretch, blinking into the new day. The trees make only soft sounds in the early morning breeze. Then the sky begins to change, almost imperceptibly: first black, then deepest blue, until finally the dawn arrives in yellow, orange, and red. The clouds seem higher this time of day, and majestic in their measured movement.

Now, my days don't start with a flurry of rushing and noise. Instead, I find a calm, a peace, a serenity that nourishes me through the busiest hours ahead.

Thank you, today, for the serenity of a new day. Thank you for the beauty of a new dawn.

Anonymous

Office gossip can zap my energy if I get too involved. I want healthy relationships with my co-workers, without falling into the trap of feeling good at the expense of others. A fine line runs between camaraderie and gossip. I can tell which side of the line I'm on by measuring the amount of time I spend in my off-work hours thinking about business. When I find co-workers living "rent free" in my head, I know it's time to detach and focus on myself. I find it helpful to inventory my own life to see if there is something I'm avoiding. I need to be willing to let go of judging and trying to control other people, places, and things. It always feels right when I return to the bottom line and acknowledge that the only person I can change is myself.

Today, I'll try to focus on myself, and avoid gossip about others.

S.C.
Dowagiac, MI

We live in a materialistic society. Every day we are bombarded by the hype of commercial advertising which drives our economy. The message that we get is this: unless we can have what's being advertised, as soon as possible, we won't be happy.

It takes discipline to quiet ourselves amidst the frenzied din of the marketplace and listen to the still, small voice within us. The message we hear then is that the most precious commodities of patience, love, and hope can't be bought. They are free gifts, available to everyone who takes the time to humble themselves and ask for them.

Today I choose to find a quiet place and listen to the voice of my Higher Power.

C.R.D.
Park Ridge, IL

God not only endowed us with the ability to think, but to choose the things we will think about. We are the only creatures in the universe so blessed, yet often we forget, letting ourselves be blown this way and that by feeling we can change if we make the effort.

Only we have the ability to reason, to analyze, and to see another side than our own. Only we can change our feelings from jealousy to understanding, from anger to compassion, from self-pity to humility. Only our brain can be altered by a sentence like "one day at a time," or "let go, let God." Today, help me to realize my full potential, to use the power of my mind for my good, to make the changes in my attitudes and thoughts that will bring me peace and serenity, and will help my clients better understand.

S.B.-P.
Houston, TX

Authority without wisdom
is like a heavy axe without an edge,
fitter to bruise than polish.

Anne Bradstreet

We counselors have such a lot of power! As authorities on this terrible disease, let us be careful never to use power for petty or vindictive ends. To never thoughtlessly reject a client. We can affirm our client's sense of value, or we can damage them with a casual joke at their expense. We can help them to respect themselves, or we can tear down their self-esteem by treating them as unimportant. We have the power to do great good, or great harm. Today, let me remember my power, and take care to use it wisely.

Anonymous

Dost thou love life?
Then do not squander Time;
for that's the stuff Life is made of.

Benjamin Franklin

Busy time seems to last the longest in memory. Weekends spent doing little speed by quickly; paradoxically, those filled with activity seem to last more than two days between Friday and Monday.

I like myself better when I'm busy and active, and I'm most drawn to vital, lively people who take this advice seriously and do not "squander time," but use it well to make each day count. Grant me the good sense to make the most of life today, to use my time well, to have something of value in exchange. Help me to spend my time, and my client's time, well.

Anonymous

I worked, once, with a very wise and dignified counselor who had a peculiar technique for dealing with stress. She kept a tin noisemaker in her pocket, and two or three times a day, when no clients were around, she'd take it out and make a silly little "cricket" sound with it. Finally, curiosity got the best of me, and I asked her about it. "My biggest fault is seriousness," she said. "I need to remember that there's fun in the world, too. So I take out my little cricket and give it a couple of clicks, and it always makes me laugh. Laughing reminds me of the fun things in life. Lets me loosen up a little, stop frowning, and start smiling."

Today, I'll try to follow her example. I'll find my own fun, and make a little noise when I get too serious.

Anonymous

As this new day begins, what is in my "storehouse"?

Is anger or resentment still burning?
Are old battles still raging?
Am I withholding forgiveness over hurts from the
        past?
Is this day out of balance, heavy on negatives?

No, today will begin with a clean slate.
I will look forward, not back.
Today, I will let go of yesterday's hurt.
I'll make the most of today and forgive yesterday's
        pain.

Anonymous

Lord, I pray for the strength to accept my limits. I can't like everyone, or work well with everyone. Once in a while, I'm assigned a client I just can't seem to warm up to. That's a real problem, both for the client and for me. Sometimes discovering why I feel that way can help me change my feelings; other times, nothing works. Then, I need help to admit my limits and seek supervision, perhaps have the client assigned to someone else.

I need help understanding that I didn't fail, that there's nothing "wrong" with me or my client. And I need help realizing that to continue together would be self-defeating; we'd both have to work too hard for little results, and we'd both risk failure. Help me to find the courage to understand my limits. Help me to turn to others for the sake of my client.

Anonymous

Confidentiality is vital to our work with clients in any kind of treatment or therapy. Without the assurance that the information they give will stay with us, clients will not reveal themselves, will hesitate to trust.

Breaking confidentiality is against the law, but worse, it's a moral crime, and can cause a client to withdraw from the helping profession altogether.

Preserving confidentiality is a tricky thing; *where* we discuss a client is as important as who we talk to.

Today, let me remember the value of confidentiality, and respect my client's privacy as I want my own privacy respected.

Anonymous

Whenever we lose something of value, we go through a process of grieving. People say, "Forget about it." But forgetting something that was once a significant part of our life may hinder our spiritual growth.

Recalling what we once had, but have lost, can actually be positive. If we lost a friend or loved one, remembering the blessing of having had that person as a part of our life, even for a short time, can strengthen our gratitude. Remembering may also help us value important relationships, to nurture them, and to develop new ones.

Even losing something "bad," like alcohol, drugs, sugar, or gambling, brings grief and pain, and it's good to remember those feelings. Forgetting the pain may cause us to underestimate the power of addiction and return to old behaviors that lead back to compulsion.

A pastor who has done extensive grief counseling uses this prayer with people who are nearing the end of grief:

"Thank you God, for all You have given me,
for all You have taken from me,
and for all You have left me."

Today, I will remember the blessings, and the pain.

C.M.
Park Ridge, IL

Today, help me remove my fears, anger, resentment, self-pity, selfishness, dishonesty, defiance, and guilt. Love me, and help me love You more. The guidance and direction to live this day, one day at a time, comes from my work and Your help. I pray for faith, love, and trust; peace, hope, and joy; honesty, openness and humility. Help me release myself from the bondage of self-will. Help my victory over difficulty bear witness to all those I would help. I pray for a sober day today, that I may help another stay sober.

Anonymous

Love turns on the sun; we have a happy day and all is well with the world.

Love brings out full size in us. It discovers within us ambitions unnumbered, goodness unlimited. It multiplies our energy beyond our imagination. It excites a courage braver than any soldier.

Love comforts like warm sunshine, refreshes like a gentle rain. Love's fire glows the longest; its arrows are the sharpest; its kisses are the sweetest; its hours are the shortest.

It speaks and hears a language known only to the heart wherein it lives.

Today, help me love.

S.B.-P.
Houston, TX

As I begin my day, allow me this moment to feel gratitude. For today I have an opportunity to be one which the miracle of recovery will pass through. I remind myself of my daily surrender, for I, too, must accept my limits. I know if I control, demand, and want it to be my way today, the miracle will not happen. I realize that today, while writing my case notes, making that phone call, facilitating a group, or listening to that patient in my office, the Power Greater than myself is working through me to offer the miracle of Good Orderly Direction. Let me be grateful today for this opportunity. As the miracle passes through me, I am strengthened to do Thy will, not mine. Let me be grateful today so the miracle of recovery can pass through me to those who need its healing power.

F.S.
Katy, TX

In the therapeutic setting, my commitment to my own program enables me to do the tasks that are at hand. As I stay centered in the Steps, I facilitate my clients' acceptance and integration of their program. My life is an example of the Twelve Steps in action, and the greatest gift I have to offer is the example of my Higher Power working in my life on a daily basis.

Just for today, I will remember to use my program to stay connected to the healing power that is within us all.

R.C.
Austin, TX

Have I enabled a client?

Have I withheld confrontation to spare my own
feelings?
Have I agreed with a statement I didn't really
hear?
Have I let my mind wander and seemed indifferent
to another's pain?
Have I short-changed someone because I was too
tired to give my best efforts?
Have I been impatient and short-tempered?
Have I withheld approval because of personal
prejudice?
Have I people-pleased, at the expense of honesty?
Have I placed my needs above my client's?

All of these can enable a client to turn away
from our help and continue self-destructive behaviors. Today, I must examine myself for potential enabling. Someone's recovery may depend on it.

Anonymous

The infant grows to a stage of unquenchable curiosity and needs to explore, investigate and question everything about himself and his environment. He identifies fingers and toes, bodily functions, and spiritual potential.

To be a successful shopkeeper, I'd have to be willing to inventory my stock and needs. And to be an effective counselor, I must be willing to undergo a regular inventory and accountability process. It's not enough to hear my supervisor's opinion of how I'm doing.

An annual retreat is a good opportunity for me to take a fearless and searching moral inventory of both my strengths and weaknesses. My clients have a right to get my best. Today, help me remember I can only give it when I'm fully aware of all I have to give, and I can only be fair when I know my own limitations.

J.B.
Pinellas Park, FL

People tend to agree that the Serenity Prayer is helpful for everyone, whether or not they are involved with Twelve Step recovery programs. It can be particularly helpful for counselors, but only if we actively use it; simple belief in its effectiveness is not enough. Often we "spin our wheels," bemoaning realities about our patients that we can't change while they're in treatment: their lack of education, or the unavailability of appropriate aftercare. Dealing with the painful realities of their lives is hard for them, but it's hard for us, too.

It's easier when we use the Serenity Prayer and literally separate the things we can change from those things we need to accept. We need to accept the fact that the client can't read or write, but we can look into alternative teaching methods. We may need to accept the fact that all the halfway houses are full, but we can focus on the client's Twelve Step involvement, and try to get him on a waiting list.

Then, as one wise therapist puts it, "Remember to leave some of the work to God!" We can get so involved with what we think is best for our patients, we forget there are many roads to recovery. We don't have future sight.

Help me today to do the best I can with the tools I have, and then "let go."

S.S.
Park Ridge, IL

*One must not always think so much about what one
should do,
but rather what one should be.
Our works do not enable us; but we must enable
our works.*

Meister Eckhart

A good counselor motivates change, is a role
model of success, cherishes sobriety, and practices
honesty and integrity. We can't become those things
by teaching them to others—we can't give away
what we don't have. We all know sad and ineffective
people who are drawn to counseling to save themselves, not others; they quickly choose another line
of work. Our clients value us for what we *are*, not
what we teach. No amount of "lip service" can con-
vince them if we don't live the principles we talk
about. Let me remember this today and never stop
"becoming."

Anonymous

A hungry stomach cannot hear.

Jean De La Fontaine

It isn't enough to teach our clients about their alcoholism or drug addiction, then send them on their way, expecting them to live a clean, healthy life. Our clients need much more: work, food and shelter, the support of family and friends, a Twelve Step program, spirituality . . . all of these are essential, too.

In helping a client fully recover, a holistic approach is needed to care for the whole person, all aspects of his or her life. Today, let me see my clients as complete people with complex needs. Let me give care to every aspect of a client's life.

Anonymous

When I am at peace with myself and my Higher Power, there's no greater force. No person, place, or situation has power over me. I will ask my Higher Power to grant me the strength I will need to be the best I can be today. I will take in my Higher Power until my whole being is filled with the strength I need to face what today has in store for me.

What have I allowed to have "power" over me lately? How can I better use the strength my Higher Power has to offer me today?

A.S.
Denton, TX

Sometimes I don't feel like I'm growing, like my life is an endless series of salutes and saying "yes" to the same old routine. My work feels like a worn puzzle with all the pieces in the same old places. I also get tired of the pick-me-up slogans like: "Feeling bored won't kill me," and "What can't be cured must be endured."

I'd like to turn that puzzle over and rearrange the pieces in a different pattern. Sometimes I find myself walking back and forth on feet that seem married to the carpet. Today, may I remember what I tell my clients: "Recovery is the experience of following through on a project, long after the mood has passed."

S.C.
Dowagiac, MI

> *"We are running shy of eagles
> and we're running over with parrots."*

Charles R. Swindall

The challenge for counselors is to be more like eagles and less like parrots. It's easy and comforting to say the same things over and over and use the same approach with every patient, to stay in the same job year after year, like a parrot in a cage.

But patients are becoming more complex, with cocaine addiction, dual diagnosis, and eating disorders the rule more than the exception. The field is expanding rapidly; many facilities are in a state of perpetual transition.

Today's counselor needs to follow the path of the eagle, searching for the truth, keeping perspective, daring to be unique in our approach to problems. We need to be open to new ideas, new programs, and new positions. We need to take risks. Our growth, personal and professional, depends on our ability to initiate and respond to change.

Today, may we have the grace and courage to soar like the eagle.

J.B.
Park Ridge, IL

"Our differences begin in sameness."

Counseling someone who doesn't share my culture is a challenge to my maturity and professionalism. In the past, I've had strong feelings about cross-cultural counseling. I've learned more about myself by being willing to accept and investigate these reactions, like fears:

—Fear of the differences I perceived in my clients
—Fear that I couldn't help this client and the client would sense my inadequacy
—Fear of the unexpected in therapy.

Supervision and increasing knowledge about the dynamics of cross-cultural counseling greatly lessened my fear. It's a relief to own my feelings of inadequacy and ask for help. Facing my fears has opened the doors to continuing realization that all human beings are basically the same in our joy and pain.

Today, I look forward to differences in my clients. Today, I will overcome my prejudices.

S.C.
Dowagiac, MI

We carry within us the wonders we seek without us: There is all Africa and her prodigies in us.

Freidrich Von Logau

The power of imagination! Where would we be without it? Imagination is hope, is change, is everything made possible. I look at clients who have lost everything, and I see them rebuild their lives. I look at one who has lost his faith, and I see him regain it. I look at one who has lost love for herself, and I see her replenish it. I see one who is at "the bottom" and I see him rise far above himself.

I see what *is,* and I see it reborn. Today, let me use my imagination to build a wonder world.

Anonymous

Each day I can touch a life, perhaps by a smile, a kind word, a gentle touch, or a warm hug.

All my counseling skills are necessary, but those skills can never replace my human compassion and my love for the human race.

I need love on those days when I get lost in myself and desperately search for "the solution." It's time to close my eyes and know that the solution is available to me.

I pray that I will always be aware of God's greatest gift—the gift of love for another human being.

K.H.
Austin, TX

Can anyone imagine a world without friends? Think of a time when burdens seemed unbearable; how would we feel if we didn't have friends on whom to unload? Friends share our troubles, but equally important, they share our joys. They hold up a mirror in which we can better see ourselves. They also allow us to be the selves we know we are but often don't want to be; they accept us as we are, and then help us to change.

Those of us who are helpers often fail to get help for ourselves, so friends are doubly important. It's great to get a hug when we didn't know how much we needed one until we got it. It's also great to have friends who make asking for hugs easier. We are twice blessed if our co-workers are also friends. Today let me try harder to make a co-worker a friend.

S.S.
Park Ridge, IL

> *"I would rather sit on a pumpkin,*
> *and have it all to myself,*
> *than be crowded on a velvet cushion."*

Henry David Thoreau

I've learned how to be alone with myself and I'm pleased to find that I like my company. Counseling takes a lot of energy; sometimes there are moments in my day when I feel drained. I've learned that solitude is my friend when I feel at my limit.

It's often hard for me to stop and take time out for myself. I have to put on a mental lampshade and forget that there's always "one more thing to do." I follow the example of a friend who was troubled by daily bouts of depression. She allowed herself 15 minutes of solitude when she arrived at work each morning. During that time, she "felt" and was "depressed as needed." Then she put depression aside and got on with her day. If the depression returned, she reminded herself she'd have time to be depressed tomorrow.

I need solitude to recharge during my day. Help me make that time.

S.C.
Dowagiac, MI

Respect your clock but never worship it.

Part of being a responsible professional means I need to make plans, set goals, and schedule my time. And there are times when following the guidelines of my schedule is a priority. But I regret that sometimes I must put a schedule ahead of a person, when a client needed a few minutes of my day but I couldn't give my undivided attention because I was caught up in a nonessential task.

People are more important than paper. Today, I will consciously work at slowing down my internal clock and give my full attention to the person I'm with.

S.C.
Dowagiac, MI

Sometimes I wonder about the word "family." Since I began counseling, I've seen so many different types. Two-person, four-person, even a 16-person family. Stepfamilies. Gay and lesbian families. It has caused me to think in much larger terms than when I first began my career.

Help me keep an open mind in working with families. Often, there are aunts, uncles, and grandparents who have been affected by one family member's addiction. The pain is usually intergenerational.

While my training has taught me much, the real learning happens when I meet with my families. Help me to look at each one individually and listen to what they tell me. They can teach me so much. Today, help me listen.

J.S.
Crystal Lake, IL

The first day of summer, and lazy warmth lies ahead. On my way to work I'll pass empty lots full of baseball, sidewalks cluttered with hopscotch and jump ropes and bicycles. Trees and bushes, fruits and vegetables are in a frenzy of production to fill their fall quota. The days are long and dawn comes with insect noises, the sounds of life. The grass grows riotously, as though there were no tomorrow. The sun takes an hour of orange and red and golden splendor to set. What a season to be healthy and sound. What a promise to bring my clients today. The joy of summer will inspire me to motivate them, as it motivates me, toward health and serenity.

Anonymous

I love a place where the wind in the pines wakes me up in the morning and sways me to sleep at night. A few times in my life, I felt an almost perfect peace. Once was in Switzerland, when I was twenty years old. Every day was full of sunshine, mountains, and blue lakes. The bed I slept in was down-filled, with white fluffy sheets. Bands played outside at night under the stars, by the edge of the lake. I remember a moment when the air was so clean and the music so beautiful, I felt almost pure peace. This memory and the feelings it brings can be a foundation for rest in my busy world.

Memories like this call me back to nature, a slower pace, and God's tender quiet found in a moment. A memory search can bring us all special foundations to rest on. Today, I will share this with my clients, so they, too, can build a special foundation.

S.C.
Dowagiac, MI

In dealing with alcoholism and drug abuse, I've found it necessary to keep things in their proper perspective. This field is unique in that the disease of addiction affects not only addicted persons, but the people they are close to, as well—and that includes me. One way to maintain my health physically, emotionally, socially, psychologically, and spiritually is to practice the principle that we are responsible *to* our clients, not responsible *for* them. Too many times I feel tense and frustrated because a client I work with is in denial. During these times, I must keep a conscious contact with my Higher Power and practice tolerance, caring, and understanding. These allow me to detach from the emotional distress my client is experiencing and regain my professionalism. When I can maintain wellness, I know I am the most effective in my work. Today, I will let go, and let God.

T.B.
Park Ridge, IL

The pain was all-encompassing. My young client, out of treatment for three months, took his own life. He was only 17 years old. I counseled the family, too, while treatment was in process, but family denial remained strong; my patient and his family refused our recommendations for recovery. The patient's father was also an untreated alcoholic. After the funeral the parents called. The father, a rugged, angry man, wanted to come and talk with me. I remember my own fears; what could I say to him? When we met he hugged me and cried. In his hand was a letter left by his son. The letter described the boy's use of drugs and the father's active alcoholism. In the letter, the boy's heart poured out in pain. The boy's father asked me, "Do you think my son would know if I went to AA today?"

Today I faced a challenge and learned that, with the pain and struggle of death, new life is created.

M.T.
Park Ridge, IL

Jill was an amateur photographer who had a darkroom in her basement. When her young son came down to play, Jill would say she'd be out in a few minutes. One day, though, the little boy announced that he'd open the darkroom door if his mom didn't come out. That would ruin the film, and Jill was up to her elbows in processing fluid, so she couldn't hold the door shut. She called to her son, who was afraid of the dark, "Don't open the door or the darkness will come out and cover you!" The little boy did not open the door.

As adults, we know better, that a door opened on darkness lights the darkness, not the other way around. Darkness can never win out over light—the light of kindness and caring, the light of love and understanding. Only when those who carry the light refuse to share it, can darkness win. Today, let me share my light with those who come to me.

C.M.
Park Ridge, IL

I respect people of principle, people with integrity, and want to be more like them. Sometimes I feel like a chameleon, taking on the attitudes and thoughts of those I'm with. I don't like myself very much, then. I want to think my own thoughts, be my own person, have my own opinions. I don't want my career to be littered with second-hand attitudes and assumptions about my clients. I want to look at the evidence, think things through, and make my own assessment of what's happening and what needs to be done. It's so easy to listen to others, to take an attitude from someone else "as is," to neglect the *work* I must do to form my own beliefs. Today, I ask for help in being a "first-hand" counselor, to believe in my own abilities and to think for myself.

Anonymous

Sometimes I can get stuck in looking for the "whys" of my client's problems. At certain stages of treatment, analyzing and interpreting are not helpful and can actually slow the recovery process to a frustrating snail crawl. "Action is the magic word," "Fake it till you make it," and "Do something even if it's wrong," are a few sayings my clients relate to. When I begin to feel like we're "on a slow boat to China," I usually need to remember those slogans and re-examine my treatment goals and plans. "Action" is often the magic word that gets the therapeutic ball rolling. My counseling seems to go better when I remember to keep things in motion. Today, I'll try.

S.C.
Dowagiac, MI

Meditation is the art of looking within—
and finding peace.

Meditation is not a "thing," it is a place inside us. Today, I will meditate. On a crowded bus filled with people, I'll "tune out" distractions to find my own special place. At work, I'll take five minutes for myself, find a quiet spot, and meditate. Between clients, I'll spend a moment in gratitude for my work and my life. At family gatherings, I'll pull back and look around, meditating on my loved ones. Today, as often as I can, I'll stop, be calm, look within, and find the place of peace I need to meditate. There, I'll find the peace and serenity I need to live this day fully, and spend every moment in joy.

Anonymous

I've learned much about the human spirit from my wilderness survival group. I was thrilled to discover this philosophy. It speaks so clearly to what I feel in my heart about the gifts and potentials of human beings. I continue to be touched by the simplicity and truth of that program.

The human condition often brings us to our knees, feeling very disabled indeed. I would like my clients to believe that their very brokenness is a noble foundation for much growth and personal discovery.

I'm grateful for any skills I've developed as a counselor. Today, I'll make a safe place for my clients to discover their inherent worth and goodness.

S.C.
Dowagiac, MI

The beginning of character building comes with doing things we dislike. There's always "an easier, softer way," but we hurt ourselves when we take it. Self-respect is built on deeds, not intentions. The best of intentions won't get us to work on time, clean our homes, teach us a trade, strengthen our bodies, or fill our pockets. Excuses are unconvincing, especially to our inner selves.

Instead, we must look at what needs to be done, take a deep breath, and plunge right in. It's harder, but oh, the rewards! Pride, a sense of mastery, the serene knowledge that we control our own lives and do not run at the first sign of difficulty. We can face the future calmly, confident we can handle anything that comes our way. Once we are master of our own character, we are masters of all the future holds. Today, let me not turn away from difficult tasks and clients, but remember the rewards that will be mine if I persevere.

S.B.-P.
Houston, TX

Some patients recover, and you never hear from them again. But our Higher Power gives each counselor a few who periodically contact us. Often, just when I've been wondering if my efforts make a difference, one of these angels will check in. The scenarios are generally similar: "I just wanted to tell you how I'm doing," or "I just celebrated three years of recovery and I wanted to thank you for being a part of my life."

These are the encouragers. They have grasped the concept of being a grateful alcoholic/addict and are living out the concept. Give yourself permission to revel in their praise of you. It's not conceit—you were placed in that person's life to help arrest the process of addiction. This client was placed in your life to encourage the work you do. One needs this inspiration to deal with a killer like addiction. The inspiration you received can spill over to the team and buoy their spirits.

Let me hear and gracefully receive encouragement today from former patients, so I may be refilled and continue giving encouragement to new clients.

L.B.W.
Park Ridge, IL

Once, I valued huge feelings. Giant loves, great hatreds, an all-or-nothing, black-or-white approach to everything. It was a dramatic existence, exhilarating and exhausting. Now I've come to appreciate moderation, for it brings serenity. Highs and lows are a natural part of life; they will happen without my seeking them out.

Taking a moderate position gives me a mellow feeling, a golden existence of quiet gratitude and gladness. Falling "somewhere in the middle," I can weigh the value of all views presented. I can appreciate all areas of the spectrum, since I'm not "stuck" at one end or another. I can love another, but don't have to take sides, to love a friend's loved ones or hate a friend's enemies. I can see all aspects of a situation, not just those I'm emotionally drawn toward. I can accept people with all their qualities, the good, the bad, the in-between. Today, I can look forward to a calm and serene day, tempered by moderation.

Anonymous

This is a day that touches the hearts of counselors — Independence Day! The day my client begins recovery, that's Independence Day. The day I turn over a character defect to my Higher Power — that's Independence Day, too. Independent of the "old way" of doing things, of running from problems, of living life in tones of gray, of having nothing to look forward to but misery and death. No more of that for us!

We're on the road to independence, my clients and me. It's an endless road, we know that, and there's no real "destination" — but the journey is incredible and gets better all the time. Today, I'm going to celebrate my independence. I've overcome a lot of obstacles on the way, and there are plenty more down the road. But today, I'm looking forward, not back. Independence, here we come!

K.I.
Chicago, IL

Whatever your special skill or talent may be, set aside a few minutes every day to exercise it. It doesn't have to be a major skill, as long as it makes you feel good. If kindness is your specialty, go out of your way to brighten someone else's life. If you're good at writing, jot down a few random thoughts to re-read this evening. If you're analytical, mentally "track down" the roots of a problem. Your self-esteem will rise, your spirits lift, your confidence renew, your enthusiasm return. We counsel our clients to find and use their talents, and we can take the same advice. Today, I will find the time to practice my skills and remind myself of my abilities.

S.B.-P.
Houston, TX

"He that can take rest is greater than he that can take cities."
Benjamin Franklin

Sometimes it takes courage to admit to others that I need to rest. The achievement-centered society I grew up in taught me that resting during the day was laziness.

Sometimes it feels great to take a rest without having "a good reason." As a counselor, I find it essential to practice the fine art of resting and taking regular breaks. When I am truly present in my sessions, I wear myself out with concentration. On some days, I go from one therapeutic session to the next without taking a break. No wonder I feel exhausted at the end of the day! I rob myself when I don't discipline myself to finish a few minutes early and make time to rest and shift gears. Slowing my internal and external pace is a soothing way to prevent burnout and other forms of counselor fatigue. Counselors who pace their days are more serene, and their healing energies are more available to themselves and others. Today, I will try to be like them.

S.C.
Dowagiac, MI

The first step towards madness is to think oneself wise.

Fernando DeRojas

Resting on my laurels, ending the search for wisdom, is dangerous for me as a counselor. If I begin to think I know everything, I will no longer confer with co-workers. I won't need to take a class, attend a seminar, or do late-night reading to understand a difficult client. I will be closed to new information, new ideas, new treatment methods. My morals will solidify, my attitudes turn to concrete, and my clients will be the poorer for it. I'll get old too soon. Help me to listen with young ears, especially to ideas that challenge my own. Today, help me to keep learning, to never think I've reached the end of knowledge. Let my mind always be open to learning.

Anonymous

May I never forget that, like my clients, I am on a journey of growth.

May I always be mindful with my clients, as with myself, that growth is a process, not an event.

I cannot give away what I do not have. It's important for me to take the time to care for my own needs. Only in this way can I hope to be of any help to my clients or those around me.

Have I taken time to be quiet and commune with my Higher Power today? Do I have and use my own resource system when I am in need of replenishing? Do I practice patience and understanding with my clients and peers, remembering it is a long process, one day at a time?

Today I will take time to do an inventory of my mental, spiritual, emotional, and physical needs. I will take care of at least one important need of my own today.

K.C.
Park Ridge, IL

When a new client enters treatment, I need patience. I have such gifts to give him—freedom, recovery, serenity, beauty, love of life—and my impulse is to give this new client all of them right now.

But that will overwhelm and confuse him. Instead I need to give out new information—new ideas, new insights—in a gradual way. This new client needs time to think. Time to absorb all this information and what I'm saying. Time to listen to himself and to think about what he's feeling. It's important that I give a new client the time he needs to reflect on the events of his past life, and to decide how he'll spend his future.

Today, as much as I want to give my gifts, let me first give time. It may be the greatest gift of all.

Anonymous

As we enter into a new day, let's consider what we are carrying that does not belong. Have we really freed ourselves from the burdens and cares of yesterday? Or are we carrying them like dead weight into today? Have we let go of pointless anger? Have we tried to forgive and forget? Or are we still cluttered with fear and frustration and resentment?

Yesterday has forever passed, and tomorrow will forever elude us. Today is the only day we have.

Today, I will try to start fresh, free of the burdens of yesterday.

S.B.-P.
Houston, TX

Sometimes we feel an instant dislike for another person, a dislike that's just not rational. We may be projecting, disliking them because they remind us of something we reject in *ourselves*. For awhile I was a secret overeater and found myself disliking overweight people. I was frightened and trying to hide my fears from myself; seeing someone heavy brought those feelings to the surface, and made me feel very uncomfortable. I responded by disliking anyone who "made me" feel that way.

Many of us are recovering from some kind of addictive disorder, and it can be painful to work with people who remind us of "the old me." But it's also an opportunity to learn a greater acceptance and forgiveness for ourselves *as we were*. Today, I pray to take advantage of opportunities for growth and to accept the person I once was

Help me to recognize my own problems, and not project them onto my clients.

Anonymous

As counselors, it's important for us to know where our inner substance and strength comes from. In our day-to-day dealings with clients, we may become too affected by the pain of their powerlessness.

Being centered means having the ability to recover one's balance, even in the midst of action. Understanding and acknowledging our need to be centered can help us weather the storms of conflict and change that are such a normal part of a counselor's work day.

Today, grant me an awareness about what our work means, as well as the purpose it serves. Being clear about why I'm doing this work and opening myself to my "Higher Power" can help me remain centered and grounded.

O.M.W.
Mundelein, IL

"A good conscience is a continued Christmas."

Benjamin Franklin

Peace of conscience allows me to fall asleep at night and be willing to put my feet on the morning floor. Nothing feels better than knowing I'm willing to do the right thing for myself and others. Today, I don't have to be perfect. I don't always take the best or right action — but I'm willing to change and try to do things differently next time.

There have been times in my life when I tried to fool my true intuitive reactions to a situation. I sometimes want the easier, less painful solution to a problem. But when I listen to my deep feelings and intuition, it seems to make my conscience happy. I pray to trust my internal "gut reactions'" today. Today, I will follow this internal prodding. I might not get what I want, but I will probably get what I need.

S.C.
Dowagiac, MI

The basis of effective counseling is simply an ability to understand people. It is an art-form of the heart; no education can "teach" understanding to one who is uninterested or unwilling to learn. Yet it's truly an accomplished art, one that depends not on the senses, but on emotions, intuition, and thought. It's an art that begins from a foundation of love and grows with time, taking study and attention to learn and refine. When we understand people, we can feel for them, and with them. When we understand the 'why' of someone's behavior, we can be objective and compassionate. We can love them even for their flaws and misguided efforts to change. The opportunities are there, all I need is a willingness to pay attention. Today, every day, help me learn understanding.

K.I.
Chicago, IL

Serenity seems to come from an underlying belief that all will be well, despite the surface "unrightness" of things. A Twelve Step Book talks of "wearing the world like a loose garment." A slogan asks, "How important is it?" Both these thoughts suggest that those everyday things, which seem so crucial at the moment, may not be so when viewed in the overall scheme of things.

Let me try to be serene today. Let me really see the beauty around me—in a flower arrangement, a lovely picture, the view from a window. Let me find a few quiet minutes for myself between sessions to reflect and shift gears. Let me take a walk, utilize a meditation book, or simply trust a power greater than myself enough to ask for help. Let me find serenity.

S.S.
Park Ridge, IL

The little child in each of us never stops needing rainbows and hugs.

> Our little child needs a safe person to sit near when tears come.

> Our little child needs to believe there are no secrets too bad to be told, and no rooms to dark to enter.

> Our little child needs to know love won't be withheld.

> Our little child needs to feel there's a path she was created to walk on.

> Our little child needs to believe he can make no mistake too bad for God to fix.

No matter how old we get, that little child lives on in our tenderest part. Remind us to clap and dance when we see a rainbow. Today, I will take time to honor the child in me.

S.C.
Dowagiac, MI

Days that are rushed and hurried, with very little accomplished, are the most tiring and unhappy. My energy falters and my self-esteem drops. What happened to me? My appointment book is filled, I have too many phone calls to make, and I seem to have lost my ability to say "no" to family, friends and co-workers.

I have let my ego push me into feeling overly important and self-sufficient, and lost some things. An appreciation of order in my life. Acceptance of the gift of 24 hours. Overwhelmed with self-importance, I forgot my mission.

To serve means asking for guidance and making order. Little meaning comes from our mission if we do not complete the task. Grant me the assurance that God has given me purpose. Teach me the real meaning of "Give me this day," and an acceptance of Your will. Help me to find order and meaning in my daily living. This good feeling will fill my spirit. As the day closes, let it close with a prayer of Thanksgiving.

L.W.
Park Ridge, IL

When my ambitions take over I can get lost in my own shuffle. Busy-sickness can cause pain and confusion. When my work is the only important thing in my life, I get off balance. Work addiction is similar to other addictions; a general definition might be: "Work becomes a problem when it creates an ongoing pattern of disruption in one or more of my major life areas." Is my physical health affected by my work? Is work the only way I validate my self-worth? Has work become more important than relationships? Do I find it increasingly difficult to take time off from work and/or "leave work at the office"? Have my family and friends complained that I don't spend enough time with them? It takes courage to evaluate my professional life. If work has become out of balance, then denial might cause me to be the last to know. Checking with others can give me more accurate information. Today, I'll aim for balance in my life. And I'll ask others for help in recognizing my out-of-balance lifestyle.

S.C.
Dowagiac MI

Industry cleans the mind, strengthens the body, guards the soul, and fills the purse. It encourages honesty and peacefulness. Hard work plants the seeds and reaps the fruit, while laziness harvests nothing. Genius is not enough; without self-discipline it is only potential. Possessions are meaningless; no one is emptier than one who has been given much, but has earned little. Industry buys a satisfaction and content that idleness can't afford. As I start my day, let me remember the value of work.

S.B.-P.
Houston, TX

Grief can feel overwhelming. It produces anxiety, fear, sleeplessness, tears, anger, loneliness, and a feeling of powerlessness. The light at the end of the tunnel seems dim. We try to fight the tears and pain, to accept anger and fear as part of the process of grief. We try to let go of a piece of our lives that we want to hold onto. Yet, for all our efforts, it feels like a cloud is hanging over our lives, and we will never be free.

But with time, patience, help from others, and a lot of work from us, the pain lessens. We find that, after all, pain is only temporary.

I pray today to remember my own grief, that I may help clients live through theirs. Give me the grace to listen and learn from my experiences: my teachers. I give thanks that pain is only temporary.

M.L.
Park Ridge, IL

What a privilege to work as a counselor. To know I affect the life of another. To make a difference in the world. Other professions may be more financially rewarding, but I'd miss the feeling of being part of something bigger than myself. When a client recovers and finds a new and wonderful life, I love knowing I was part of that process. That I played a part in helping someone be reborn.

Losing a client is hard, of course. But as counselors, we know we're playing with huge stakes: life itself. We can't "win them all," addiction is too powerful an enemy.

But we do win some, and that joy makes up for the losses. Today, I give thanks for the privilege that's been granted me. I give thanks for being a counselor.

K.I.
Chicago, IL

The young person soon learns that to have social ties and relationships, he or she must assume responsibility. Must work to be part of the class. Must pay dues to join the club. Must practice to be on the team.

It's not enough to be aware of people. Each of us must act on that awareness; communicate our appreciation.

It's good for me as a counselor to listen. I can help my clients in a non-directive way as they disclose themselves. Often "the healing is in the telling." But I must also help clients to solve problems. It's in this area that I must be most responsible. Today, I will open my ears to others.

J.B.
Pinellas Park, FL

Today, one day at a time. After that counseling session, I sat back to process my thoughts and feelings. I must slow my tendency to quickly write my notes, and take a moment to call upon my Higher Power for a true assessment of our counseling session. There is often deeper meaning to my interactions with my clients; may my assessment lead me to help my patients find their special purpose. Without purpose, they will have difficulty making sense of their suffering and pain. The plan that we make together gives them direction on their journey. As I go through my day and write my treatment plans and progress notes, let me take time to call upon my Higher Power for guidance in my assessment and clarity in my planning. Today, let me remember that, with the guidance of my Higher Power, I can walk with my patients along their journey and help them find their special purpose and direction.

F.S.
Katy, TX

I feel more content in my counseling chair on return from an adventure. What a joy to discover myself a good traveling companion. I always yearned to take risks. When I was a child, I dreamed of traveling through the "Dark Continent," fascinated by tales of Africa and the mystery of the Congo. My dad told me, "Be careful," and "Don't be silly." Gradually, my risking spirit became tamed. I discovered ways to risk that brought more pain than adventure.

Now, in the second part of my life, I'm embracing the child in me, saying "yes" to adventures inside and outside. I'm thrilled to know that there's a walking route to the top of Mount Kilimanjaro, and that the scent of Easter lilies perfume the springtime air of Bermuda.

Today I'll remember that the more I accept and nurture the adventures inside and outside me, the more I can appreciate the potential, dreams, and visions of my clients.

S.C.
Dowagiac, MI

The balance I need most is getting away from my safe little world and spending time with people and activities not "in the field," or "in the program." I need my support group, and I love my work. But I need other interests, too. I need to risk doing things I'm not very good at. To try out new ideas, enjoy new experiences. I need to stop thinking and analyzing. I need to spend time with people who are *already* healthy. I need to lighten up, to laugh a little, to be silly sometimes. It's an old saying that "variety is the spice of life." My work is so serious, so important, that when my day ends, I need all the "spice" I can find. The sights, sounds, and adventures of the world await me today—let me be brave enough to take advantage of them.

Anonymous

Think of yourself as a source of energy—
even more—as a channel of energy. The life force
that animates us doesn't come from any human
source, it comes from our Higher Power. If we stay
close to our Higher Power and keep the channel
open, that power will flow through us. We are ideas
in action, works in progress, striving always to
achieve more, to become more. Today, let me be
open to the life force in me and around me.

S.B.-P.
Houston, TX

Help me today to understand that addiction is a *disease*. To better learn to act, not react to its disposition and rebellion. Help me to help our patients to help themselves. I pray today for them, for myself, and for all those suffering outside.

I want to be able to "buy what I sell," one day at a time. I can do it with the guidance of my Higher Power. I Thank Him for today, and for the opportunity to serve others in His name.

B.L.
Birmingham, AL

She has slipped! Give her courage to come back to us, though the path back is vicious and twisted—the loneliest place to be. I pray her Higher Power finds her, as mine found me when I slipped. Grace was extended to me, and will be to her, through surrender. I pray that she hits bottom fast—before she dies and is lost. We won't give up, ever. She *is* me. Having been in that place of hell, with no direction, I thank my Higher Power for sending one of your children to save me and redirect my path to sobriety. I pray she is saved, too, before it's too late.

J.C.
Denton, TX

When I get too involved with a client, it's hard to stay objective. Pretty soon I'm so absorbed in my feelings that I'm not sure whether I'm helping or hurting. Some clues let me know this is happening. One is that I begin to avoid confronting the client, or begin to feel protective. Another is feeling pity for him, rather than having compassion. I hear myself think of someone as "poor So-and-So." That means I'm in trouble and need to regain my perspective. I'm blinded by my feelings and can't do this client justice. Addiction is a deadly disease; while I'm feeling sorry for a client, that client is not getting the help he or she needs to recover.

Today, I will pay attention to my inner feelings. If I'm over-involved, I'll pull back and regain my objectivity.

Anonymous

One of my fellow counselors often quotes this favorite saying. "Lord, don't let me see myself as I see me, for I'm not that bad. Don't let me see myself as others see me, for I'm not that good. Lord, let me see myself as you see me — for that's the way I am."

To paraphrase this in my counseling, "Lord, let my patients know the real me, for that's exactly what they are getting; and when I am wrong, help me to be prompt in admitting it."

Maturity comes with forming positive habits that ensure good relationships, determining helpful choices, and avoiding unhealthy activities.

Humility is truth. It's a realistic and healthy appraisal of my strengths and my weaknesses. It's appreciation of my own talents and gifts, with an active acceptance of my limitations and mistakes. Today, I'll be humble.

J.B.
Pinellas Park, FL

To the anagrams we use, I'd like to add S.S.S.—Sit Still and Suffer. Suffering has gotten such a bad name lately, as though it's some shameful thing that one should never experience. Who told us life must always be great? That everything we want must be ours? That the rain will wait until we're under a tree? Fact is, life can be boring, life can be unfair, life can be cruel. Sometimes, for no reason, things go wrong and nothing helps. Maybe it's time to just get through it. Like the rain, the feeling will pass. Like the season, things will change. And we'll be stronger for it — we've survived a problem. We *can* experience pain and disappointment, and live. Our hearts may break — but they keep beating. Today, I'll stop demanding perfection from an imperfect world filled with imperfect people.

K.I.
Chicago, IL

When things go wrong, I need an ant, a garden, a tree, even a weed to look at. It's easy to get lost in the wonders of nature, and troubles fade away.

The fragile velvet of a flower petal is vibrant with color, perfect in symmetry. What elegant sculpting there is in the veins of a leaf, leading from the plant's heart to the smallest cell. What variety there is in the bark of trees—the smooth silk of birch, the crusty elm, the reptile of pine. There's miniature glory in a busy ant, bustling back and forth from here to there, blissfully unaware of me and my giant problems (and my giant feet).

Today, when things go wrong, give me a bit of nature to help me find perspective. Today, let me be alive to the beauty in the small creations of the world.

K.I.
Chicago, IL

How quickly one learns that effective treatment of addicted people and their families requires a *TEAM* of professionals. No one discipline, educational background, or experience can adequately respond to the complexities and hidden corners of this illness. Just as we know a patient can't be treated in isolation from the important people in his life, so we know a single counselor can't be the only vehicle of healing energy. My *TEAM*, therefore, allows me to fulfill my deep-rooted commitment to give the best service possible to those still afflicted.

Today, I am grateful for my team members.

K.L.
Park Ridge, IL

In our daily work with alcoholics and drug abusers, we emphasize the importance of pursuing pleasurable and relaxing experiences. But do we emphasize these in our own lives? Do we have leisure time? Do we routinely scrutinize the quality of our leisure lifestyles?

There are more hours of leisure in our lifetime than there are work hours. How are we using these leisure hours to grow and develop into whole, spiritual, healthy individuals? If we give leisure more meaning in our lives, we "allow" ourselves to become whole and well human beings.

Today I will take time for myself for meditation, exercise, or reading, and grow "at my leisure."

C.W.
Champaign, IL

The best part of working with people is their wonderful unpredictability. We are so different one from another, so endlessly surprising. It's easy to stay fresh when working with people. The search for understanding is never over. About the time we think we've figured it all out, we meet a client who has a new and different set of character traits, in a completely unexpected combination. Five minutes ago, we thought we were experts—now we're students again, learning and re-learning our craft.

It's humbling, aggravating, humiliating on occasion, but never, ever, boring.

Today, I look forward to my work with excitement. For the sake of my clients and myself, help me achieve humility. Let me be open to new ideas. When I'm confronted with my limits, help me not resist change. Grant me the grace to be open to new growth.

Anonymous

Caregivers are often serious-minded people. We may feel we deal with nothing but people's problems—that we get our "highs" from being constantly in crisis. We may complain that we're always tired and have little energy for anything but our work.

Perhaps we need to ask ourselves how long it's been since we've had fun, or done something really frivolous. We may be like the recovering person who feels too tired to go to a Twelve Step meeting, but finds he's revitalized when the meeting is over. If we agree that "all work and no play makes Jack a dull boy" but don't have time or energy for play, the answer may be that we don't commit ourselves to *making* time for play.

Today, I'll examine my priorities. I'll remember that people do the things that are important to them. What things are important to me?

S.S.
Park Ridge, IL

Before practicing the principles of our program we lived our lives "upside down." We measured our self-worth by what we imagined others thought of us. This became a major driving force in our lives. We became defensive and tried to hide even our most harmless errors for fear of being found imperfect. We went to any and all lengths to please others, but failed.

But how we feel about ourselves comes before how we feel about others, which comes before how others feel about us.

Our program shows the way to live "right side up." It reminds us to first love ourselves, before we can love others. Our self-esteem is a gift which we need only to accept and use on a daily basis.

Help me today to nurture my own ego, and not use my clients to help me love myself.

J.C.
Moorestown, N.J.

Reaching out and asking for help is difficult for many of us. We need to feel competent and in control; we fear rejection, are too proud or stubborn to simply ask. Or so we think. Surprisingly, the problem is often something quite different: we may be having trouble knowing what to ask *for*. Is it a simple, reassuring hug we want? Or something to soothe away all our lifetime of fears? Do we want help with an errand today? Or expect someone to take care of us for life?

Expecting too much of ourselves and others eats away at our self-esteem and self-respect. Being unclear about what we want makes asking for help a threatening experience. The more clearly we know what we want in specific, here-and-now, concrete terms, the easier it is to ask for help and get results. Today, I'm asking for help to figure out what I really want, and if my desires are realistic.

D.M.-L.
Marblehead, MA

There is never, ever a justification for gossip. It damages everyone involved, especially me, if I'm taking an active part. It makes me feel small and petty and mean to express anger, resentment, hatred for someone else, and to do it in such a guilty, cowardly way—behind their backs. I'm deliberately, with malice aforethought, hurting another person, and for such a shabby reason. To feel superior at someone else's expense. Or to "go along with the crowd," people-pleasing my way to self-disgust. My Twelve-Step programs calls this, "Making points for myself by taking them away from someone else." A good description. Gossip is hard to resist, especially when I'm feeling needy. But today, it's a temptation I'll try to resist with all my might. Help me to see the good in people, to speak as well of others as I'd want them to speak of me.

Anonymous

We're saddened when a client has a relapse, a "slip." But it's important to examine those feelings. Are we concerned with the pain of the client? Or our own hurt pride? Are we feeling the client's pain? Or our own? It's easy to feel let down and betrayed when a client relapses. Self-pity comes fast, because we spent time and effort in helpng him or her get better, and it didn't pay off this time. But addiction is very powerful, and recovery can be a long, hard process. Some of our greatest successes stumbled a few times on the road to recovery. I hope, today, to think through my reaction to a relapse. I pray to hurt for my clients, and not myself. Help me to value them as the changing, growing people they are. Help me to keep trying, no matter what happens. Help me to keep loving them. I pray that this relapse will lead to real recovery.

Anonymous

Eddie came by last night on his way to a Twelve Step meeting. He "graduated" from treatment a few months ago, and he's doing just great. He's so clean he gleams, and he has the eyes of a man in love—and he is in love, with sobriety.

I hugged him, we all did, and then we stepped back and said good-bye as he left for his meeting. It was hard to let go. I wanted to become his sponsor, to exchange phone numbers, to pull him aside for a long, joyous talk, to hear every detail of his life since he left, to invite him over for dinner.

But I held back. He has a new life now. We helped him achieve sobriety, our job is finished. He needs to meet new friends, find new heroes. Time for us to let go. Still, Eddie lives on in me.

Today, if I'm feeling frustrated or blocked, I'll think of Eddie. My heart will rise and I'll remember why I love my work. Even when it means letting go.

K.I.
Chicago, IL

Before my morning meditation, I often awake feeling fearful, reluctant to get up and face the day. Often I feel unable or incapable of doing what needs to be done.

My clients and I walk similar paths. But they walk their paths with even greater fear, more misgivings, less self-confidence than I.

To deal with my life appropriately, I turn to my experience of recovery, my relationship with my Higher Power, to the fellowship of the recovering community, to the Twelve Step programs, to my reserves of personal health, and to my professional competence, discipline, and skill.

In order to deal with their lives, my clients can turn to me, and through me, have access to my experience, strength and hope.

Help me to remember that I am not God. Help me to remember that I, too, am one of your children. Help me extend to others the grace that has been granted me.

J.S.
Rockford, IL

Perfectionism is a burden that keeps me from you.

Isn't it great not to have to be "the perfect counselor" today? Isn't it freeing to accept my humanness and the possibility that I might make a mistake today? It's been said that a growing counselor is someone who can say, "I was wrong." Learning to be wrong and forgive ourselves plants the seeds of tolerance and understanding for our clients in their very real humanness. A "perfect" counselor is very hard to sit with in therapy. How can I relax and watch the tapestry of therapy unfold when I have rigid expectations of myself? When I must be perfect and in control? There are no ways to hide from clients my personal rigidity and expectations, and they become powerful monsters when I bring them into the counseling room. Today, I'm grateful I don't have to be "perfectly therapeutic."

S.C.
Dowagiac, MI

As a manager, I'm constantly dealing with all-day problems: within the organization, with staff, with clients. I try to listen closely and help facilitate successful resolution of problems, but the problems often overlap—and they never stop!

I frequently end up taking those problems home with me. There, "the problem list" seems to grow as I respond to the needs and concerns of my wife, my children, and running a household. Recently I found myself very short-tempered. My problem-solving skills were diminishing. *I* was becoming a problem! Then I realized I was simply exhausted.

We talk about helping our clients create balance in their lives, but my life was becoming unbalanced. I needed time to "do nothing!" I began taking 20 minutes in the morning and late afternoon to meditate. Today I will remember I'm worth taking time for myself. As a result, I will have more time for others.

S.H.
Park Ridge, IL

Have I grown too impatient? Do I want the people around me to grow, improve, or get better at my own pace? Do I push, pull, and force, without accepting limitations?

In my obsession for instant recovery, do I forget to validate the tiny steps, the small triumphs?

In my quest for excellence, am I becoming ineffective?

It is only by appreciating where others are coming from that we can help them grow.

Today, I will not measure others by my ruler. I will commit to appreciation of others at the level where they are. I pray for understanding, patience, and an open mind.

B.G.
Hialeah, FL

Each is given a bag of tools.
A shapeless mass and a book of rules;
And each must make; ere life is flown,
A stumblingblock or a steppingstone.

R.L. Sharpe

Do I use the tools and rules of my profession to help others? Or do I enable others to remain unchanged?

Do I work hard to continue my education? Or lay back and continue in ignorance?

Do I actively practice my skills? Or rely on easier methods?

When my counseling days are over, will I be remembered as one who made a positive difference? A negative difference? Or no difference at all?

Help me today to remember all the tools I can use in my work. Help me to make my life a stepping stone for others as they pursue recovery.

Anonymous

The gentlest counselors I know are also some of the toughest. Sometimes I see my interior life as a large room that needs a good sweeping on a regular basis. When I let my own pain, anger, and unfinished business fill me up inside, I lose some of my capacity to understand and feel compassion for my clients.

I believe that every human can be honestly validated and affirmed for having their own special goodness and worth. In my meeting with clients, I am an explorer, discovering goodness and gifts to share. I have learned about their need for validation from myself: when I feel esteemed and validated by you, then I can handle the hard truths you find in me. I can open myself to learning only when I feel safe.

Help me to build a safe place for my clients today.

S.C.
Dowagiac, MI

Have I become a tough, hard, insensitive counselor in order to survive? Is being a counselor a role I play without thought or feeling? Is it getting easier to confront than to support? If I stop seeing the pain around me, will I be blind to the joy, too? If I see a patient as only a set of limitations, will I reach far enough to enable growth?

Today, I'll try to care enough to experience disappointment. I'll accept that the process of recovery is hard and difficult, but the benefits are worth it. I pray that I may show my sensitive side and that others might benefit because of it.

B.G.
Hialeah, FL

On a just-rained afternoon, I saw the sun set in gold and red and a touch of blue. It took my breath away and I stood, entranced. If only I could see everything with that same awe-struck wonder. Sometimes, I don't even look. Or I look, but see instead what's inside; the worries and concerns of my day veil the beauty of the world. Today let me look outward, and not inward. Let me see all of creation with eyes of wonder.

The beauty in a care-worn face, the spark of hope in every client's eyes are there for me to see. Today, I will look.

K.I.
Chicago, IL

In order to be a true "helper," we must, first, be able to put ourselves in another's place, to feel what another is feeling. Only then can we understand what another's life is like, what battles she is fighting, what forces are at work in her, what burdens she carries. And only then can we help her to find a new way to live.

Sometimes, empathy is hard to find. People seem so different, one from another. Yet we *are* all the same. We all feel hunger and fatigue, we all grieve at loss, rejoice over good fortune. We all need to love ourselves, and we all fail. We all need help.

Today, I'll try to look beneath the surface, to find the sameness, not the differences, between others and myself. I will try to feel *with* others, and not risk feeling against them. My family, my co-workers, my clients—all need my empathy. Today, I will try to be there for them.

S.B.-P.
Houston, TX

Working with a resistant client, I sometimes imagine the therapeutic process as a tiny seed buried under concrete. Slowly, gradually, with pressure so small it can't be measured, the seed pushes its way up. Slowly, gradually the concrete gives way, a little here, a little there. Soon a green shoot pops through, and leaves begin to stir and unfold.

Counseling can be like that. Slowly, gradually, almost invisibly, I counter his resistance. With minute reassurances, I build a foundation of mutual respect and trust between us. Subtly, I use my professional tools to challenge, to nurture, to confront.

Against the odds, like that seed, we succeed at last, breaking through the concrete of denial, to breathe the fine air of freedom and begin the journey of recovery.

Today, I'll remember the incredible power of that tiny seed. I'll persevere for me and my clients.

K.I.
Chicago, IL

Lord, make me an instrument of thy peace.
Where there is hatred, let me sow love;
Where there is injury, pardon;
Where there is despair, hope;
Where there is darkness, light; and
Where there is sadness, joy.

O Divine Master,
Grant that I may not so much
Seek to be consoled as to console;
To be understood as to understand;
To be loved as to love
For it is in giving that we receive;
It is in pardoning that we are pardoned; and
It is in dying that we are born to eternal life.

Is my life out of balance? Do I give without receiving in turn? Have I forgotten to recharge my emotional energy on a daily basis? Am I under the assumption that my title of "counselor" exempts me from the needs of a human being? Have I become prey to the "super person" syndrome? Do I see my needs as weaknesses to overcome?

We all need love, warmth, joy, and fun to grow and develop as individuals, even counselors. If we fail to nurture ourselves, we have little to give away.

I will aim today to fulfill responsibilities to myself. I will not forget for one second that my personal life needs my love and attention. I pray that I may be as caring of myself, as I am of others.

B.G.
Hialeah, FL

"Sleep on it," they say, and somehow it works. No matter how troubled I was at night, no matter how many anxious minutes or hours I spent worrying over a client, somehow I wake calm and easy.

Sometimes sleep has brought solutions to the problems of the night before. Other times the problem remains unsolved, but after a good sleep, I somehow don't feel as anxious about it, as pressured to find a solution.

This is magic! No one seems to know just how it works, whether our unconscious works a problem through, or our Higher Power sends blessings of peace in the night. Whatever tools are employed, it *does* work, and that's good enough for me. No matter how difficult my caseload today, however hard life may seem, I will rest assured, and sleep will help with my problem.

Anonymous

He was no different from any other human being except he had a disease he just would not accept. With tears in his eyes and half-soured hurts curdling his soul, he cried, "But I don't want to be an alcoholic. I feel like a failure." How sad that he saw himself as a failure because he had this disease, even though he'd not chosen to become alcoholic.

Using that same yardstick, are we to feel like failures because we contract ill-health, or experience life circumstances beyond our control? Is it failure we encounter on our life journeys, or unwillingness to accept those very human, unchangeable realities?

Being a failure does not come from outside, but from our own willingness or unwillingness to accept realities about ourselves. Are we willing to embrace the unpleasant realities that confront us? Our Higher Power, who has embraced us in all our realities, has the power to give us daily serenity. Are we ready and willing for God's embrace, so we might embrace ourselves? Help me to embrace my own realities and debilitations. Let me love and accept myself.

R.H.W.
Park Ridge, IL

Have I forgotten to learn from the people around me? In my quest for objectivity, am I closing myself off from the experience of the patients I see? Have I stopped listening? Worse yet, have I stopped growing? Every recovering addict has some message to share. Any human interaction has the potential of being an enriching moment or an empty gesture. It is our choice that makes a difference.

I will try today to listen with a third ear. I will be in tune with the people that surround me and will grasp every opportunity to learn, to grow. I pray for receptivity so I may receive as much as I give away.

B.G.
Hialeah, FL

We all recognize bluster and self-righteousness in others. Sometimes we catch a glimpse of it in ourselves. But we don't have to look too deep to find faults behind the boasting. We can't help but wonder if false pride isn't just a cover-up for a truer self-estimation.

If we don't feel small in the face of the Grand Canyon, a beautiful sunset, or a stirring piece of music, we've lost perspective on ourselves. We have also lost the ability to appreciate the marvels of the world.

When I look at the sky which You have made,
at the moon and the stars, which You set in their
places —
what is man, that You think of him;
mere man, that You care for him?

As we shape our own lives, we carry on the work of creation. We can take no credit for the beauty around us. But today we can give expression to the beauty within us.

T.N.
Park Ridge, IL

The journey into myself is an exciting part of being a counselor, and often the most educational. When I learn something new about myself, I have another tool, another insight, to help me with my clients.

The reverse is also true: when I learn something new about a client, I learn something about myself, too. I begin to notice that behavior in myself, but now I know what it means and I can choose to counteract it.

What a happy bit of luck — to work in a field that gives me such opportunities for personal growth! I'm grateful for that. I wonder what I'll learn today?

Anonymous

When we stop changing and growing, we begin to die. This is especially critical for people in recovery and for those of us who work in the helping professions. Recovering people may relapse . . . counselors may burn out.

As the recovering addict needs to take a daily inventory, so we counselors need to inventory our burnout tendencies. If we're working harder but enjoying it less, we may need to look into a creative solution. How intriguing it is that the solution harks back to willingness to change.

Today I'll examine my burnout quotient. I'll talk to others and get feedback if I need it. Above all, I'll check to see if I'm doing the same old thing, over and over again, in the same old way. If so, I'll find ways to make my work more creative.

S.S.
Park Ridge, IL

It's hard to live honestly and happily with friends and family when we aren't open about our needs. A hidden agenda puts the burden of our lives on others. When we want something, do we let others know? None of us can read minds. No one knows our feelings until we share with them. When we tell others how we feel, we may be pleasantly surprised by the response.

None of us should have to fumble along in ignorance, trying to guess what a loved one needs. When we're open about what we want; no one is trying to guess our secret, and resentment doesn't build. It's hard to be vulnerable, to openly reveal our needs. The risk of rejection is scary. But only by taking that risk and sharing our feelings can our needs be understood and met. Today, let me be honest about what I need from others. And let me encourage others to be honest with me.

S.B.-P.
Houston, TX

"H.A.L.T." tells me to slow down and take my personal daily inventory.

As the pressures of caring for others begin to affect me, let me not forget to make sure I take time to feed my *H*unger.

How well I care for my body will affect my feelings of *A*nger and my need to control others.

I must seek patience and tolerance, and not allow myself to get too *L*onely. My relationships and willingness to share with others keep me in touch with reality.

If I get too *T*ense or *T*ired, I must remember that my Higher Power is always there to support me, to give me rest and relaxation.

As I begin or end my day, let H.A.L.T. be a part of my continued personal inventory.

F.S.
Katy, TX

Like doctors and lawyers, counseling should be called a "practice." We surely do practice our skills; in fact, that aspect of our work is one of the major joys. We're always "practicing," never "finished." Human beings come in such variety, such an infinite number of styles, that we never need reach an end of learning, and the boredom that results. No two clients have the same thoughts and behavior in the same combination. No two respond to the same counseling techniques in the same way.

So, the "practice" of counseling constantly challenges our expertise and offers endless chances to develop and satisfy our curiosity.

Today, I give thanks to be part of "the practice of counseling."

Anonymous

People sometimes say, "It's OK to talk to yourself, but if you start giving yourself answers, you're in trouble." But self-talk can be a very useful tool for recovering people. Many of us suffer from a negative self-image. We've told ourselves we don't amount to anything, we don't measure up to others, or that we just can't cope with life. We tend to reject praise.

We need to learn to accept positives from others, and learn to give them to ourselves, and one way is using self-affirmations. Deep-down, we seem to know we're unique, special, worthwhile people, but we tend to keep that buried, often under the guise of humility. We need to list some affirmations and say them to ourselves on a daily basis, until we really believe them. An example might be, "I am lovable and capable," or "I am trusting myself and going at my own speed." Only when we can accept ourselves as we are, can we change.

Just for today, I will affirm myself. If others don't give me the strokes I need, I will give them to myself.

S.S.
Park Ridge, IL

A young person instinctively becomes social and wants others to enter his life. He wants to belong, to be a member of the club, the gang, the team, the class, the group. It's human nature to gain social awareness and begin a lifelong selection of other persons.

It's so important in our recovery and maturing to renew our social awareness. Every good feeling or positive experience in our life will have some connection with other people, with the dynamics of love.

As a counselor, let me be aware that the pain of my patient may be from an unmended relationship. Help me to view the Human Ecology of that person.

J.B.
Pinellas Park, FL

Like every other professional, counselors are only as good as the tools we use. Education is surely critical, to teach us the ins and outs of addiction.

But some of our best tools are unusual ones. Compassion helps us avoid hurting another unduly, even in the interest of recovery. Empathy lets us feel *with* another person. Intuition gives us information we can't get from books. The ability to endure another's pain keeps us from enabling or becoming hardened. Honesty with ourselves and others provides a foundation of serenity and respect. Self-love keeps us from destroying ourselves in the process of helping others. A belief in the basic goodness of others gives us hope for what could be, rather than just what is. A sense of perspective helps us set priorities. Forgiveness keeps us from being judgmental with ourselves or others. Dedication keeps us trying to help even when we're discouraged.

An odd assortment of tools, but they work! Today, I'll try to remember all the tools I have, and use them well.

Anonymous

Whatever a growing child discovers in his world and surroundings or finds out about himself, talking about the experience is instinctive. How often have you heard from children, "Look what I found!" "Guess what I saw?," "D'ya know what I did?"

Talking about problems can be healing, too. The wisdom of the Twelve Steps suggests how well this healing process works. As a counselor, I'm in need of this healing. The more I listen to others telling of their hurt and pain, the more I need to learn to do the same.

Today let me remember that I cannot expect anything that comes close to rigorous honesty from my patients unless I am willing to be rigorously honest myself.

J.B.
Pinellas Park, FL

My prayer for today is that I not forget my team members, and not take them for granted. With so much energy directed toward our clients, it's easy to neglect my comrades in arms. I'm grateful for them, and I ask to become more responsive to them.

Help me to give credit generously and with a happy heart. Help me applaud someone who performs better than I do, and not feel resentful. Help me to overcome my competitive drive, to work *with* my team members, rather than competing *against* them. Help me appreciate them, and work to have them appreciate me. Let me be helpful, rather than bossy. Help me to learn from them, instead of demanding that they learn from me. Help me appreciate, every day, how much each contributes to our total effort. Help me appreciate how special they are.

Anonymous

Nothing feels better than having my feet on the ground! Growing up in an alcoholic family, the ground was always shifting; it was hard to feel rooted. I learned to be a "dancer" long before I learned to be a counselor. I lived in the highs and lows of yesterday and tomorrow as I danced and struggled from one trauma to the next. "Balance"—what a novel concept! "Keep your lows high and your highs low"—you've got to be kidding! Wouldn't life be boring if I found a way to stop the spinning and live in today?

Over the years, I've developed the art of being bored; boredom is more like a necessary part of balance. It's really the lack of excitement and external stimulation that allows me the peace to sit still with myself and with my clients. I believe this quiet contentment is the best spiritual gift I've ever been given.

Today, I'm grateful that I have developed a decreased tolerance for excitement and, on most days, "I've got my feet on the ground."

S.C.
Dowagiac, MI

Prejudice reaches farther than assumptions based on race or religion. The word itself means "pre-judge," to assume that someone has certain characteristics based on an external, rather than an internal, criteria. I pre-judge someone as poor if she's shabbily dressed. I pre-judge someone as a business man because he's wearing a suit. I pre-judge someone as stupid if he uses rough English, or as intelligent if she speaks well. I pre-judge someone as "good" if they appear friendly and harmless, as "bad" if they appear menacing or unkind.

These pre-judgments may seem trivial, but in fact they're dangerous—because I may never look past the outside to see the person who lives inside. And I may not get to know someone wonderful, because I didn't look close enough to recognize that hidden value. I don't want to be judged by my appearance, and I don't like myself when I judge others that way.

Stopping pre-judgments isn't easy. But little by little, starting today, I'll try.

Anonymous

In my quest to facilitate recovery, I must re-member that each client must ultimately find his or her own way with the help of their Higher Power. For only that Higher Power knows the past in its en-tirety; the things that brought my client to this time and place. I need to be aware that my ideas about a person's growth may be only my personal judgment. I need to continually hold my perception of these things up to the light of prayer, remembering that my own shortcomings can confuse my views.

Today, it's my responsibility to keep working my own program. It's my job to strive to improve my conscious contact with the God of my under-standing.

D.N.
Fox River Grove, IL

*True happiness is of a retired nature, and an
enemy to pomp and noise;
it arises, in the first place, from the enjoyment of
one's self;
and, in the next, from the friendship and
conversation
of a few select companions.*

Joseph Addison

I find myself suspicious of those who too
loudly proclaim their happiness. Instead, I'm at-
tracted to the gentle smile, the shining eyes. These
declare more loudly than words that happiness lives
within. My happiest moments seem to be quiet
ones: watching children on a playground, finishing a
much-loved book, a moment of meditation in the
midst of a busy day. At times I feel I can't hold so
much joy. And if I catch a glance at myself, I see
that light shining from my eyes, too. The light of
real happiness. I pray to be worthy of these moments, and to find them today.

Anonymous

"The essence of genius is to know what to overlook."

William James

The truly wise people in my life have been gentle with me. I had a counselor who seemed to have eyes in the back of her head. She always seemed to understand the part of me that was afraid. She knew just the right time to be tough and honest with me, and when to "overlook" things I didn't feel worthy to bring out in the open.

This sensitivity is one of the best gifts of love I've been given. By respecting my needs, she helped me to feel worthy and lovable. I could share my secrets and fears when my inner resources were ready. I learned that guilt is when I feel I've made a mistake; shame is when I feel I *am* a mistake.

I pray to have this respect for my clients, to provide a safe climate in which I'm kind and sensitive to the heavy burden of shame that is often brought into the therapy room.

S.C.
Dowagiac, MI

An injury is much sooner forgotten than an insult.

Earl of Chesterfield

Working with addicted clients calls for great sensitivity. These people are hurting, but they show it in confusing ways. Denial can make them hostile, manipulative, overly fearful, disspirited, even violent. Above all, they are sensitive to us. We have great power, yet we work under pressure and stress.

We may forget how a casual slight can hurt. We may forget how terribly vulnerable our clients are, how needy for our affirmation of their value.

Today, let me be aware of the pain my clients feel. Help me to be aware, always, of their feelings. Help me to think before I speak and act. Help me to bring affirmation, not pain, to my clients.

Anonymous

One very real paradox for counselors is this: the expectations set by our supervisors and ourselves must be high — yet we need to avoid perfectionism. For many of us, especially those in recovery, the struggle against perfectionism is on-going. Our fragile self-esteem gets such a lift when we do a good job, when we feel effective and creative, when we are helpful and useful.

How can we find a balance? How can we take care of others, but still take care of ourselves? How can we allow ourselves to make mistakes? The answers are in some basic concepts. We need to take inventory of ourselves regularly, and be honest if we're trying too hard. We need support and feedback from our peers, and we're responsible for requesting it. We can benefit from looking at our motives: do we genuinely desire to help those we work with? Or are we looking for approval from others? Finally, we need to regularly ask ourselvs if our hard work with our clients is doing more harm than good, by helping them avoid responsibility for themselves. Help me to find that balance.

S.S.
Park Ridge, IL

I need to remember that my clients need me—my attention and awareness of them—even more than the words I say. I may be the first person she's tried to trust in years; it's important that I let her know I value her, even if she doesn't value herself. The lessons I teach about alcoholism and drug addiction, the example I set in my own program of personal recovery, my professional behavior—all are important. But most important, most necessary of all is my unspoken attitude toward this client. I must attend to what he's saying, what she's doing, how he feels, how she's changed since our last session. My attention can't wander inward, to my own thoughts and feelings. I need to make eye contact, to say, "I'm here with you, right now, where you are."

Today, let me remember that "being there" is just as important as teaching.

Anonymous

For more power, develop more patience. Patience brings optimism to sickness, calm to calamity, and perseverance to poverty. Patience is unrestrained by intolerance, unmoved by reproach, unshaken by disaster, unbent by persecution.

Patience creates faith in a power greater than ourselves, harmony in the family, success in business.

Patience cools the anger, bridles the tongue, restrains the hand. It endures hardship and builds anew.

Patience looks to a new day with trust, and awaits the dawn with serenity.

Patience has such power, let it work for me today.

S.B.-P.
Houston, TX

So many of us struggle with perfectionism that it seems to be a universal problem. Why do we try so hard to be perfect? Because we crave approval from others? But it can also be a way to avoid taking risks, or a way to feel sorry for ourselves. If we can't be the best at something, we avoid even trying to do it. Heaven forbid that we should be mediocre! Or, if we try and aren't perfect, we can justify feeling miserable. It often seems the pleasure we seek comes from the perfection itself, and not the simple joy of doing any task "the best we can."

One way to combat perfectionism is to realize that "a desire to please Him does indeed please Him." Our Higher Power, whatever we choose to call Him, knows we're human. Our attitude is the important thing, and the direction in which we're moving. If we want to change, if we're working toward recovery, it needn't matter that we make mistakes along the way. Indeed, we must encourage human frailty, give ourselves permission to make mistakes.

Today I'll allow myself to be less than perfect. I'll try to do the next right thing, and not worry if I don't do it perfectly. I'll remember that I'm human.

S.S.
Park Ridge, IL

Fall starts today. Such a vital, invigorating time of year! It's hard to sit still with so much just outside the door. The trees are turning on their charm full blast, a last surge of color before winter. The air has a special tang you can almost taste. Pumpkins and trick-or-treat are coming soon. Frost glazes the grass early and late. Hot chocolate warms the evening. The nights are cool, curtains blow in the breeze; it's bliss to snuggle in a warm bed. Heavy jackets and plaid flannel shirts come out of hiding. There's so much to enjoy this time of year — no wonder it's the season of thanksgiving. I'd love for my clients to be well enough to enjoy all this. That, this year, they'll have reason to give thanks. With some help from us, the miracle can happen. As I prepare for work today, I pray the beauty of the season gives them another motive for recovery.

K.I.
Chicago, IL

"Easy Does it" is a Twelve Step slogan I teach my clients, and it's a good one to use for myself, too. I need to take it easy when I'm not the perfect being I sometimes demand of myself. To be easy with the frailties and foibles and humanity of myself and others. To accept what *is*, rather than demanding that things go the way they "should."

Life goes better when I'm easy, and I find better solutions. Fretting won't shorten the grocery line, but when I'm calm I can relax while I wait. When I'm at ease, the days are smoother, my heart is calmer, I like myself better, and I'm better liked. It's lovely to trust in myself, to trust in friends, family, and co-workers. It's comforting to do what I can to change the world, but accept my limits with serenity. Today, no matter what frustration comes my way, no matter how difficult things may be, I'm going to take it easy.

Anonymous

In the helping fields, there are many different models of treatment, but one theme common to all is that no one can recover alone.

While I work in this field, I need support, too. But it's hard for me to reach out for support. I'm readily available to support others, but feel a little uncomfortable asking for or accepting help when I need it.

Recovery programs are spiritual in nature, and it seems that the spiritual principle of "I" (myself alone) becoming "we" (myself and my Higher Power) is as essential for the helper as for the client. Some cases and problems are very stressful, and can drain the energies of any counselor.

At these times, we need to practice humility and reach out for support. And we need to be aware of support we can give to teammates. It's true, "we keep what we have by giving it away." Today I'll remember that I don't have to be alone.

J.B.
Pinellas Park, FL

The most frustrating clients for me are those who use hostility to resist recovery. At those times, I try to remember what I heard once from a very wise counselor, who said, "It's the disease talking, not the client." It's so easy to forget that simple fact, to lose our objectivity and take things personally. As much training and experience as we've had, a difficult client can still "push our buttons" if we're not careful. But, "It's the disease talking, not the client." That little phrase has helped me regain my composure and recall the goodness that is in every client. Like tarnished silver, the sickest client can be aided with affection, education, counseling, and hard work. As I prepare my day, let me remember how easily my "buttons" can be pushed if I'm not careful. Today, when I encounter denial, hostility, violence and people-pleasing, help me to remember that, "It's the disease talking, not the client."

Anonymous

Self-pity is like a snake, and it can wrap around my life. Self-pity is a subtle enemy, and often I find it hiding under my pain. When I feel "stuck" in a problem, self-pity is often the glue.

When I discover in myself a pattern of negative reactions about work and feel unappreciated, I need to look deeper at my attitudes. Do I depend too much on others for approval, become stuck in discouragement and self-pity when I don't get the praise I feel I deserve?

When I constantly *look* for praise, I never get enough. It's certainly nice to be affirmed by my supervisor and co-workers, but waiting for the approval of others can be a suspicion-building and depleting experience. Today I'm challenged to claim and personally acknowledge my own gifts as an effective, growing professional. When my worth is affirmed from the inside, there is little room for worry and self-pity.

S.C.
Dowagiac, MI

I was in a meeting recently that re-taught me a difficult lesson to learn. A new group member was there, and I felt instantly uncomfortable with her. I perceived her as very strong, sure, and judgmental. I decided to avoid her, not caring to deal with such a personality.

The comments went around, and she put in appropriate, but rigid comments here and there. My opinion of her, begun with a first impression, became set.

Then it came her turn to speak, and I was startled to see the strength gone, replaced by fear and uncertainty. She seems honest, and very human. This was a surprise to me, because I'd already decided she was different.

Today, I wonder how much I've missed by entertaining prejudices. Keeping an open mind is vital. There will always be those who "rub me the wrong way," if I let myself judge them. Insight is so very different from misconception. I need to be willing to see the person God is forming. Oltherwise, I cheat myself and those I come into contact with. Today, I'll try to see past first impressions.

D.N.
Fox River Grove, IL

Human beings are dynamic, always moving, acting, changing. We may move toward good, or we may move toward destruction, but we are never, ever static. With my own recovery, I'm always moving either in the direction of getting better, or I'm moving toward relapse. I can keep it simple then by asking myself, "Am I going in the right direction today?"

A client, too, is always in a state of change. I must keep my wits and skills about me to help them move in the right direction. They won't stop changing when I'm inattentive or careless—but they will stop healthy change. For my clients, I ask myself today, "Am I aware of the direction my clients are going? Am I available to help them move toward wholeness?"

J.B.
Pinellas Park, FL

A wise set of books I read many years ago taught that love is letting go of fear. The more I learn to be unafraid of me, the more I can love you. Counseling challenges me to be entirely separate from my clients, but at the same time be connected. The part of me that must always remain separate has to do with my own ego needs; expecting my clients to fill any of those needs diminishes my capacity to view them objectively. The knowledge that I'm a good counselor will come from my supervisor, my clinical team members, and myself. Not my clients. If I look to them for affirmation, I might find myself saying what they *want* to hear, instead of what they *need* to hear.

I pray to keep my ego needs separate from my counseling. I pray that I never need to see a reflection of myself in my clients.

S.C.
Dowagiac, MI

A counselor friend and her husband spent a recent winter afternoon catching snowflakes and running to view them on a microscope slide before they melted. Like the individuality they saw in snowflakes is the individuality I see in my clients. When all of my clients start to sound and look alike, I know I'm the one off balance. When I step back and regain my own personal balance and perspective, then my clients again become their own unique, individual selves. This uniqueness makes my work a daily adventure. What a joy to meet the person who walks into my office for the first time. I try to maintain a feeling of respect for my clients and a belief that their lives can be better. I don't ever remember meeting a client who was "hopeless." I'm grateful today to have the continuing opportunity of communicating hope to clients whose pain and remorse have distanced them from their internal healing potential.

S.C.
Dowagiac, MI

My anger is a signal to me that I've heard something that displeases me and my pride has been ruffled. I wanted to be perfect, but another person has pointed out a character defect. I wanted to be humble for all to see, but my self-centeredness has been exposed to the world.

Having prayed upon waking for God's will this day, it's been handed to me in the form of constructive criticism. Now, I must recognize my anger for what it is, and make a positive change. In this way I'll grow, one day at a time.

Help me to use my anger as a flag of attention, to help me recognize Your love and care in the form of beneficial comment from my fellow man.

J.W.P.
Moorestown, NJ

Counseling is a cerebral profession, and at times it's exhausting. When I get too much "into my head," when I'm worn out from thinking, it's a great relief to look to nature for simplicity. To take a walk on a tree-lined street. Stare into the bright face of a flower. Be soothed by the tides. Awed by a night sky.

Nothing is so healing, so refreshes the soul, as time spent with nature. In the light of such beauty, the problems of the world seem less harsh. Pain and depression, poverty, and misery are eased when I look on the majesty of nature. My weary soul soars like an eagle, communes with the trees, frolics like a new-born puppy.

Help me to remember how much beauty awaits me, if only I will search for it.

Anonymous

"Better bend than break."
Scottish Proverb

Learning how to compromise is a necessary skill in alcoholism counseling. Alcohol brings people to their knees. When a client "hits bottom," the emotional and physical scars feel soul-deep. A counselor is often the first one at the scene of the "bottoming out." There's an urge to confront at this time, but the best treatment I know for these clients is what I would want: dignity. All of us have dignity, but our dignity is most buried when we are at our lowest point. Then, we need someone to grant us a bit of dignity, a way to hold our heads up — even an inch. A way to "save face," to make even a small choice, to hear a word that dispels shame. I believe these are the finest therapeutic gifts a counselor can give a client. Sometimes we must bend and compromise, withhold confrontation and truth in order to bring these gifts. But "saving face" may be the beginning of recovery for our clients.

I pray never to forget how to bend and be tough at the same time.

S.C.
Dowagiac, MI

*When you know a thing, to hold that you know it;
and when you do not know a thing, to allow that
you do not know it — this is knowledge.*

Confucius

Saying "I don't know" can be hard. But as a
counselor helping others to change, I must know my
limits or I can't learn more, or won't seek help when
I need it. There is no shame in being "stuck."
Rather than letting false pride get in my way, I
should be ashamed *not* to ask for help when I need
it. My clients rely on me to give them the best
counseling I can, even if that means turning to another for help.

Today, I ask for the knowledge to realize my
limits, and the courage to admit them.

Anonymous

It's hard to admit I need help, that I'm stuck. I want to be a Super Counselor, faster than a speeding Big Book, able to leap tall problems at a single bound. But I'm just a human being, with all the frailties, contradictions and failures of my species. Expecting perfection from myself is false pride at its worst. That attitude will stop me from acknowledging problems I can't solve; without the help of others, my clients, could suffer from my ignorance. False pride can jeopardize my own recovery program, too. Demanding perfection means constant failure, and that might be too hard to bear without some kind of "instant relief."

Today, I ask for help. To put aside false pride. To admit defeat. To know when I need help. And to accept myself as I am, even though I'll never be "super" anything.

K.I.
Chicago, IL

Always on the lookout for defenses in my clients, I need to monitor myself, too.

Like repression: do I hold back feelings that scare me? Am I afraid to confront myself and others? Denial: am I seeing things as they really are? Or through a veil of egotism? Displacement: I'm yelling at one person, but am I really angry with someone else? Reaction formation: do I give preferential treatment to clients I don't like for fear they'll "find out" how I really feel about them? Rationalization: do I justify my mistakes with "rational" excuses? Or admit them and learn from them? Projection: do I reject in others what I can't accept in my own character.

These defenses are dangerous for my clients, and for their counselor, too. As I start my day, let me remember that I can't help others if I'm not healthy. Help me to recognize and work through my own defenses, as I do those of my clients.

Anonymous

Once in a while (not often, thank heaven) a violent client gets past the screening process and "loses it" on the unit. This is awful for everyone involved, frightening and disturbing. We all suffer from it, the other clients, and staff.

It's hard at those times to realize that the violent client is suffering so much. That's hard to remember when I'm scared. It's frightening to see someone lose control in that way. I feel protective toward the other clients; I want to shield them, not only from the possible effects of the violence, but even from the sight of it. It takes all of us a while to get over an experience like that.

Today, I'll try to forget my own feelings and pray for that client, whose pain is so great that only violence can express it. I pray that he gets the help he needs to find recovery, and peace.

Anonymous

Before I leave for work today, please help me to resolve my resentments. To remember that I love this profession, even with its heartaches and frustrations and setbacks. Help me to solve my own problems, rather than blame others. Help me to avoid martyrdom. To remember that I am there for the sake of the clients — they are not there for my sake. Help me to take whatever action is needed to change my life, instead of wallowing in self-pity. Help me to remember that taking care of myself, getting enough sleep, eating right, and attending to my spiritual growth will help me avoid and work through resentments before I'm overcome. Help me to look for, and find, the good in those I meet.

Anonymous

Every day I work in the field of alcoholism. Yet, when I'm touched by the results of addiction in my own family, I become blind, oversensitive, hurt, and confused—usually all at the same time.

I become resentful that my family members are unable to talk, feel, or trust. I react with anger or impatience when they become preoccupied with persons or objects.

Will I ever learn? Today, let me begin by paying more attention. Let me see and hear clearly. Let me give my family the same compassion I give my clients.

P.Z.
Park Ridge, IL

Difficult clients are my teachers.

Learning to "keep it simple" can be a very valuable therapeutic tool, especially with difficult clients. Sometimes I tend to overcomplicate my work and look for puzzles that aren't there. Sometimes I find myself living in my client's *problems*, instead of the solution. Certain clues let me know I've gotten off base:

> "daydreaming" ahead of where my client is
> checking the time
> doing most of the talking
> wanting to interrupt and give the "right"
>   interpretation
> breathing more heavily than usual
> feeling anxious to fill the silence
> feeling defensive
> questioning my counseling abilities

Remembering to keep it simple and trust the process allows me to "return" to the therapy room with my client and reconnect with all my sense. Sometimes just being truly "present" is the best therapy. Today, it's my place to begin.

S.C.
Dowagiac, MI

When today ends, what will I have made of it? Will my work bring me satisfaction and pride? Or emptiness and self-disgust? Will my clients benefit from my presence? Or be left unmoved? Will my teammates think of me with gladness? Or indifferences?

When my life ends, what will I leave behind? Will the world be better for my efforts? Or worse? Or will I be forgotten entirely?

Help me to remember, today, the impact I have on others. Help me not put off doing the things that will fill my life with gladness.

Anonymous

A parable I read in school helps me face days when I feel bankrupt, inadequate, tired, or just not up to par, and especially when I feel ill-equipped to face eight hours of counseling:

> A saintly man was asked by his priest to go to a nearby town and help the people there solve their many problems and improve their lives. The man was afraid of the task. "I have so many weaknesses, such limited knowledge," he said. "How can I help others?" The priest smiled, patted the man on the back, and answered, "All you need do is bring a little love there."

No matter how much I fear not having enough to give, one thing I can always do is "bring a little love there." Help me to do it today.

J.B.
Pinellas Park, FL

Prayer is a source of strength that never leaves me. The comfort of my Higher Power fills my life with serenity and peace.

Last thing at night, before drifting to sleep, I spend a moment thinking about the events of my day. I think about what I did wrong, what I did right, what I'll do differently (and better) next time. I feel forgiven for my mistakes, and praised for my accomplishments.

First thing in the morning, I spend another moment or two with Him, preparing to embrace this new day. I think about my clients and co-workers. I plan something fun for the evening. I thank Him for another day to be alive.

I don't know how I ever lived without the strength and serenity of daily prayer. Now I can't imagine life without it. Thank you for this most precious gift.

Anonymous

I love my special friends. Their eyes reflect hope to me during difficult times when I feel like I'm down for the count. My friends have been there for me in the midst of my private gales.

Ever since I was little, I've cherished and guarded my friends. To me, nothing is as comforting as sitting with a "safe" friend and pouring my heart out without having to censor my words. I'm grateful to have several safe friends in my life today. Others are scattered across the U.S., and I connect with them only rarely. Yet when I do, it feels the same; yesterday easily becomes today. I like to feel that I'm a good friend, as well as a good counselor. Nurturing friendships give me energy and insight to work more productively.

Today I'll be grateful for my special friends and the anchor they give my heart.

S.C.
Dowagiac, MI

*"The real voyage of discovery consists not
in seeking new landscapes, but in having new eyes."*

Marcel Proust

When routine settles in or a heavy workload continues with no end in sight, the day may seem gray and unexciting. Frightening questions come to mind. Can patients get well? Will the situation ever change? Have we stopped growing? Can fulfillment be achieved in our current work situation? Is it time to move on?

But is feeling so discouraged actually a subtle temptation to respond to a "geographical cure" and run away?

It's easy to identify and talk with patients about their escape attempts. We help them to stand still and look within, sometimes for the first time. When they do, they often discover their full potential, the wholeness that was hidden in their disease.

Like them, we can respond to our personal unrest by standing still and focusing within, and seize an opportunity to uncover the wholeness within, that generates creative energy and joy.

What will we see today in a quiet moment? It may be a new vision, a new energy for the 'now.'

E.M.
Thornton, CO

I learned a lot about the pain of alcoholism from the homeless. I saw human brokenness and solitude that was incomprehensible, but I found some peace in my work when I stopped trying to figure out the "whys." Then, I could see individuals grasping to hold on to dignity. The homeless create their own special subculture, and work to care for each other. I'll never forget a picture that was sold up and down the street to the "tourists." It touched my heart. It showed an elderly man sitting on the curb of a city street, his head bent. A shopping bag held his belongings. Under the picture was printed this message:

> *"The streets are so narrow*
> *and crowded with hunger*
> *that there is no one here who*
> *remembers the sea . . . ."*

(Author Unknown)

Today, let me remember the homeless client, who no longer remembers the sea.

S.C.
Dowagiac, MI

Help me today not to rush my clients through their grief. Every change we make in our lives results in grief. Let me be aware of the loss felt even when giving up destructive things like alcohol, drugs, food, a lifestyle, behaviors, friends, or thoughts. Loss of any of these will bring on grief that will have to be worked through slowly and carefully. There are many methods for working through grief, but it cannot be rushed. Let me not demand that my clients rush through grief too quickly, before the work is really finished. Pain can make me uncomfortable; help me not to belittle their grief because of my own discomfort. Help me give my clients enough time to let grief become a healing process.

Anonymous

How often we get angry and frustrated at patients who are in denial, at family members who resist recovery. We work and work, try harder and harder. We get tense and tired. We feel inadequate.

If we're fortunate, a seasoned counselor will say, "You're doing all the work!" And the key to letting the patient do the work is accepting the patient. We need to see each with fresh eyes, and see who they are—not who we want them to be. We need to look through and beyond the defenses—the hostility, fear, anxiety, or humor—and see the suffering person who has come to us for help.

When we recognize their humanity, we can be clear in our role. Our job is not to "fix them," but serve as a guide, showing them the way to recovery. When we do that, we often end up receiving more than we give.

Today, I will accept people as they are, and be with them.

J.B.
Park Ridge, IL

Letting go of a challenging client is so hard! I drive home thinking about solving the riddle. What steps can I take tomorrow? What reading will help? Which co-workers can help me gain insight? But as I approach my exit on the freeway, I make a conscious effort to put all that behind me. It'll wait until tomorrow. Now, my family needs me, all of me, my attention and affection. And I need them. As that exit approaches, I begin to relax, to feel my mind and body "let go" of work. I think about dinner, and what the children were up to today; how my spouse and I will spend the evening. I think about a hot shower and comfortable clothes and being surrounded by happiness. But letting go isn't easy. Today, as I begin my day, I ask to remember that there is a time for work and a time for my family. Let me give my best to each, and let go gracefully.

Anonymous

No rock so hard that a little wave
may beat admission, in a thousand years.

Alfred, Lord Tennyson

There are some things in life that intuition tells me not to give up on. Sometimes it urges me to continue with a project long after practicality tells me to quit. I get restless, frustrated, and uncertain when I feel I'm going in the right direction but can't find the end of the path.

To continue to grow and learn professionally, I need to persevere. Some days, I would like to rest on my laurels and not tackle any more big learning projects, but my intuition often has other ideas. Professional perseverance helps me keep developing my gifts and talents and explore new horizons.

I believe I will know when I reach the place professionally where I should be. My intuition will tell me; it will feel right. Today I will walk my path with the faith that it leads me where God wills me to go.

S.C.
Dowagiac, MI

To be an effective counselor, it's necessary that a response to a situation be appropriate . . . that's simple enough, right?

However, a therapist must be aware of the complexity of a patient to facilitate appropriate, simple actions. Then, the patient must be helped to consistently choose simple actions in response to maddeningly complex personal issues.

"DON'T DRINK. READ THE BIG BOOK. GO TO MEETINGS."

In order to live successfully in recovery, we must be able to respond to complexity in simple ways. The Twelve Step program, a relationship of grace with one's Higher Power, personal spiritual fellowship, the mentoring of sponsorship, and a balanced lifestyle respecting the need for abstinence from mood-altering substances . . . all this, complex as it may seem, is simple . . . "one day at a time." Help me remember simplicity today.

J.S.
Rockford, IL

The quality of our recovery depends on how we love ourselves. A positive cycle is created when we get closer to God and ourselves through others. There are days, though, when our attitudes, beliefs, and behaviors wear away at the foundation of our own recovery. What a subtle process! It may begin with a series of thoughts: "I'm inadequate, unworthy, unlovable . . ." These messages produce destructive attitudes; soon we find ourselves needing relief.

Will we turn to our old ways of "running," and avoid reality through chemicals, relationships, food, money, work? Or will we put our tools of recovery into action and break the cycle of destruction?

Today I will remember that my happiness is related to how I love me. I will ask for help to love myself as I am loved.

A.S.
Denton, TX

Being in a care-giving profession is rewarding for me, because I'm quite talented at giving care. *Receiving* care, though, can be difficult. Sometimes a feeling of guilt or selfishness overcomes me when I allow myself to be cared for. This is very self-defeating.

Just as I've had to practice giving care, I need to practice receiving it, especially from myself, my most constant companion. Often I catch myself judging or speaking harshly to myself. Would I talk to a friend that way? Would I hesitate to love, comfort, or pamper someone I love very much? Of course not! I need to apply the same treatment to myself that I would my dearest and closest friend.

Today I'll make a list of things I'd gladly do to help a close friend. Then, I'll choose at least one item from the list and allow myself to receive it.

A.S.
Denton, TX

There are two things I can change — my own attitude and my own behavior. I am responsible *for* me. I am responsible *to* my patients, co-workers and others in my life. If I can remember this simple fact today, I'll allow a great burden to be lifted from my shoulders.

Many times I feel frustrated or inadequate when a co-worker, client, or someone else in my life does not meet my expectations. I can help myself and others by taking good care of myself, so I'm able to give what I can without *feeling responsible* for their attitudes and behavior.

I pray for guidance in understanding the difference between being responsible *to* others, and responsible *for* others.

A.S.
Denton, TX

I like the sparks of adventure that I see in my clients. When gently fanned, these sparks help someone sense their individual energy and gifts for life.

A senior citizen named Sam taught me a lot about adventure. When my children were small, we lived near a nursing home. During one of Sam's regular "escapes" from the home, he met my three girls. They promptly led Sam, wearing his pajamas and traveling hat, into the kitchen for milk and cookies. Sam's visit became a ritual that summer; we even began buying extra bags of cookies.

My girls and I enjoyed Sam's gusto, and looked forward to his "escapes." Sam eventually got too ill to "escape" very often, but his spirit of adventure and zest for living remained with us.

I like to believe that there is a little bit of Sam in each of us. Today I'll try to nurture that spark in myself and my clients.

S.C.
Dowagiac, MI

Today as I work with people afflicted by the
disease of alcoholism, I pray that God helps me recognize the difference between helping patients
through the change process and imposing my will on
them. I recognize that *my* will has nothing to do
with their recovery. I'm merely an instrument of
God, helping people through their own discovery/
recovery process. I am willing today to turn my will
and my life over to God as I understand Him, and
trust that He will assist me in making the best decisions for my patients and their families.

D.N.
Park Ridge, IL

New counselors enter the field with much fervor and sometimes unrealistic expectations. A few relapsed patients later, the counselor may begin to doubt his or her abilities as a helper.

At this point, one must come to grips with addiction and chronicity. Addiction: being unable to discontinue a practice, though it is harmful to myself and others. Chronicity: continuing a destructive underlying process which appears to be arrested. As counselors we must remember that we were placed here as instruments to interrupt that destructive process, not totally stop it. Alone, we are no match for chronicity. That's why group recovery is so important to the recovering addict.

Counselors need to remember that single-handed attacks on alcoholism and drug abuse are rather fruitless efforts. But the use of a team approach is far more effective for both the patient and the helper. Take advantage of your peers on the treatment team. Use team meetings to talk openly about frustration and discouragement. You'll find you're not alone. Guidance and support will be available to you. All you have to do is ASK for it.

Grant that I be a team player and not a discouraged, lonely, falling star (hero).

L.W.
Park Ridge, IL

Out of bed, get dressed, drive to work, good morning, it's staffing and a report on all the needs and actions of my clients. It's another day, and I think, where am I? Where am I going? Then, as I look at my schedule, I stop and remind myself that I'm a messenger, a listener, a unique medium by which my clients will discover themselves today. By my presence they may awaken the spirit of love and value that lives in them. If I can recognize first my own specialness, I will then be free to allow them their time. As I begin my day I'll remind myself of my value, my self-love, my willingness to meet my clients "where they are at." I'll walk with them on their journey toward wellness.

Let me take this moment to recall my specialness, my uniqueness. Let me be grateful for the opportunity I have today to help guide those I meet from sickness to wellness and spiritual recovery.

F.S.
Katy, TX

Tomorrow is Halloween! What a fun time, especially for children. They dress up in costumes to fool you, and wear masks: masks to tickle you, masks to scare you. Half the excitement of Halloween is in guessing, "Who's behind that mask?"

Our clients often wear masks, too, pretending to be one way but hiding the real self. It's our job to help them come out of hiding. But fear and pain accompany the smallest attempt to remove the mask. They have such fear of rejection "when you see what I'm really like," and pain in facing the reality of their lives.

Help me to be gentle as I encourage clients to lift the mask that keeps them hidden from those who care. Help me be aware of the fear, and the pain, that they feel. Today help me encourage someone to find the good person who is hiding beneath the mask.

T.G.
Park Ridge, IL

I have the best job in the world: helping clients (and myself) change in a joyous way. That's the good side of the coin. The flip side is the drudgery of paperwork. When I'm with a client, time seems to fly. But when there are forms to fill out, I keep checking to see if the clock's been unplugged; it hasn't moved a centimeter. When I'm with a client, my patience is endless. After fifteen minutes of paperwork, I'm ready to do something else. When I'm counseling, I'm alert and excited and fulfilled. When I'm charting, my eyes feel heavy, my mind too fuzzy to concentrate.

Help me today to remember the importance of all aspects of my job. Help me remember how critical documentation is to our field, and to tame my restlessness. Help me to remember that I agreed to perform the whole job—not just the "fun parts." Help me learn self-discipline, to enjoy the parts I like best and accept the rest with good grace.

Anonymous

"All work and no play makes Jack a dull boy."

Many who work in this field have a well-developed compulsive facet of their personalities. This trait is a double-edge sword. Because of it, we usually provide efficient, effective care to the addicted person. But compulsivity can also become a millstone around the counselor's neck. It can drive us to always go one step further, take care of one more detail, until we are exhausted.

Counselors need a healthy balance between responsible clinical coverage and compulsive overwork. A hobby is one way to develop and nourish this critical balance. Most counselors are blessed with a creative spark; it's important to use this for ourselves. Drawing, writing, painting, knitting, sewing, reading, woodworking, collecting and restoring items, any handiwork. For me, working with a piece of wood is very refreshing. It lets me to express physical energy and helps me distance from work so I can maintain a healthy perspective. It frees my mind to access a new clinical approach.

Teach me to relax the clinical vigil. Help me develop other meaningful activities in my life today, so I can be a more effective counselor.

L.W.
Park Ridge, IL

Today, we can be thankful for friends. Friends to laugh with and cry with. To talk to and listen to. To share all the highs and lows of life.

Having friends enriches us beyond words. We come to rely on the support, the affection and the shared moments, good and bad. It's great to have a partner to share triumphs, someone who is happy for us when things go well, who hurts with us when things are a mess. Time spent with a friend seems to fly past, leaving memories that sustain us through the hardest times.

Being a friend enriches me even more. There's a sure, sweet joy in saying just the right thing to help a friend feel a little better. It's wonderful to feel needed and know I can fill the need. To make someone's life a little better, just with my presence.

Help me to be a good friend today.

Anonymous

Step Twelve says, "Having had a spiritual awakening as the result of these steps, we tried to carry this message to alcoholics, and to practice these principles in all our affairs."

This spiritual awakening seems to be simply a product of self-realization: "I'm okay. I'm no better or worse than anyone else. I do have something to give. I've come from the dependent stance of 'I need you' to the awareness of 'I love you.'" Today I will remember my greatest asset and strength as a counselor is contained in that awakening. It lies in being just me. I have to be me.

J.B.
Pinellas Park, FL

Life is uneven; it has its ups and downs. Days of exaltation are followed by days of despair. Sunshine alternates with shadow. Some days are too short, others too long. There are valleys to travel, and mountains to climb.

It's easy to get frustrated with this changeable life. But maybe we need the differences to fully appreciate what we have. If every day had sunshine, pretty soon, ho hum, another sunny day, how boring.

And it helps to remember that bad days are offset by good days. Sunshine still follows the rain.

As a counselor, remembering this helps me "let go" of a client's relapse, to think about all those who are still strong in their recovery. Our failures help me appreciate our success stories even more. Today, whatever I encounter, I'll enjoy the variety of life.

S.B.-P.
Houston, TX

"It's okay to plan — just not to plan the outcome."

Anonymous

Before involvement in a Twelve Step program, my planning often included deciding on a specific outcome, usually only one, thought to be "the best." If that outcome wasn't achieved, I felt too disillusioned to recognize any good that resulted from this altered plan.

But through a Twelve Step program we learn that when events occur through God's will rather than our own, the unexpected outcomes that occur bring benefits we couldn't have planned within our human limitations. We learn that it's important to plan, but our attitude must be open and flexible to new results. Only then can we provide room for God to help us achieve the outcomes that are truly best for us.

Help me to foster an attitude of flexibility and openness in my planning, and to rely on Your grace for the best outcome.

A.S.-T.
Park Ridge, IL

Have I forgotten how to laugh? Is my daily life completely permeated by the seriousness of this fatal disease? Have I lost the balance I fought so hard to achieve? Has life turned into a struggle, a burden I have to bear?

I need to remember that sometimes only humor can help us from one crisis to the next. It's the caring jest that many times breaks denial more quickly than the serious jab.

Today I will laugh. I'll certainly laugh at all the silly things, at some of the serious ones, and most of all, I'll laugh at myself. I pray for humor and lightness of heart.

B.G.
Hialeah, FL

My patients are doing well in
treatment. They talk about their
addictions. They're getting honest.
They take risks. I feel great! I'm
super-counselor!

My patients are unmotivated. They
deny their addictions. Tell half-truths.
Refuse to share feelings. I feel
terrible. I'm a lousy counselor.

As I read my diary, I see the word *"my"* too
often associated with patients. Are they *"my"* patients? If they belong to me, I have control over
them—and must also be responsible for their recovery or their relapse.

Have I become confused about my powerlessness? Have I allowed the responsibilities of my
position to lead me into believing I am God?

I return once more to the Serenity Prayer—
"The courage to change the things I can"—that's my
behavior. "The serenity to accept the things I cannot
change"—that's other people. "The wisdom to know
the difference." God grant me serenity, courage,
and wisdom.

J.M.
Katy, TX

Addiction is like an iceberg: most of the symptoms and problems are unseen. As a counselor, that raises a serious challenge. Most clients present a denial that's very hard to break through. How difficult to work with someone's problems when they refuse to admit those problems exist—even to themselves. So our task is to help each client learn how to look beneath denial and find the truth. How much are they drinking or using? What serious problems has their alcoholism or drug addiction caused? What do their family and friends feel about their chemical use? And then we repeat, and repeat, until truth is found. As each question is answered more and more honestly, a little more of that iceberg is revealed. Until, finally, denial is broken and recovery can begin.

Today, I won't be discouraged when faced with the task before me. I know that, like an iceberg, the full scope of the addiction is *there*—I just have to look deeper to reach it.

Anonymous

There is only one way to solve problems: to face them honestly and confront them head-on. Running away won't work, or trying to squirm around and under them, or pretending they aren't there or never existed. You have to plow straight through problems, live straight through them, until you come out the other side. This is persistence. It takes courage to confront problems, a clear eye to face the facts, and a clear mind to do the next right thing. Persistence may be the most necessary human quality of all. Today, I will try, and try, and try again to solve my problems. I'll make persistence a part of my own life, for myself and as an example to others.

S.B.-P.
Houston, TX

Do all the good you can,

By all the means you can

In all the ways you can,

At all the times you can

To all the people you can,

As long as ever you can.

John Wesley

It's a great privilege to dialog with another human being in "listening love." In counseling, we have this opportunity each day. We're excited to be learning so much about our role in the dialog, and we have available many ways to listen. Do we "listen" with our eyes, our hearts, and our guts, as well as with our ears? Do we listen for what is unsaid, as well as what is spoken? Do we listen with compassion? Without judgment?

A dialog done in listening love is intimate. What a wonderful adventure to intimately participate in the journey of a fellow soul. Do we sometimes feel the awe of God's presence in our work? Do we sometimes pause internally in our sessions and "bless the moment"? Today I'll be aware of my Higher Power working in my counseling sessions, helping me hear my clients with listening love.

S.C.
Dowagiac, MI

Once I thought every problem required a solution, that every argument had to be resolved by agreement on both sides, that one of us had to give in. I'd argue and discuss, fight it out, thinking every battle must be won. Now I know that, sometimes, it's best to "agree to disagree." Harmony doesn't mean there's complete agreement on an issue—it means everyone is content with their feelings and those of others. I like this. You can have your ideas, I can have mine. It brings great serenity, agreeing to disagree. When my friend likes apples and I like oranges, we can leave it at that. What a great relief to learn that not all battles can be won, or are even worth the time and energy to fight.

As the day goes by, let me rejoice in the differences of others, and remember that harmony lives *in* me, not through agreement from others.

Anonymous

Help—I'm too busy—I'll do it tomorrow—forget it—I'm lost—I'm scared—nobody makes it—what's the use? I stop to close my eyes, to feel and hear the voice from within. It quietly calls out to me: Relax, Easy Does It, One Day at a Time, First Things First.

These words I've heard over and over until they've become a mantra that helps me clear my mind. I'll stop now, for a moment, and say them slowly to myself. Relax . . . Easy Does It . . . One Day at a Time . . . Let Go and Let God . . . First Things First . . . Relax . . . Easy Does it . . . One Day at a Time . . . Let Go and Let God . . . First Things First.

As I work today, let me not forget these words. Help me remember the calm and peaceful voice of my inner child, nurtured by myself and those I love. Today, I'll take time in my hectic schedule to listen to my inner voice, where my Higher Power nurtures me and those I'm with.

F.S.
Katy, TX

My office is near a lake, and every spring, the ducks take over. They waddle slowly and happily in small circles, at perfect peace with their world. Ducks know how to relax! Ducks don't hurry, they take it nice and easy. A mother duck slowly leads her line of new babies across the road, and the cars line up and wait. We smile, slow down, and accept the pace of our feathered friends.

I have a lot to learn from these ducks. Sometimes I get so overworked, so rushed, I forget the lovely healing gifts of nature and the seasons. Somehow I can't imagine ducks racing about, forgetting how to be ducks. Why is it so difficult for me to consistently nurture my human need for balance, peace, and relaxation?

Life is short. In the "light of eternity," I have a lot to learn from ducks.

S.C.
Dowagiac, MI

Holiday seasons can be especially stressful for recovering people. One reason is we tend to think of holidays as magical, mystical, times and set unrealistic expectations. Holidays may also bring to mind memories—pleasant or unpleasant—of indulging. For many people, facing holidays without drinking, drugging, or overeating may seem a dreary, unfulfilling prospect.

Some advance planning can help. We can attend more meetings and spend more time with friends in the fellowship. We'll need to be more aware of slogans like "Easy Does it," and "One Day at a Time," and use "H.A.L.T. to remind ourselves not to get too hungry, angry, lonely, or tired. We can plan to do some things we enjoy, and take time to be good to ourselves. Or ask others how they manage holidays safely, and be alert of parties within the program. Above all, we can make a point of finding the beauty, joy, and love in any festive season, and ask for help if we need it. Whatever methods we use, sobriety or abstinence should be our first priority.

As holiday seasons approach, help me not to expect too much of myself or others.

S.S.
Park Ridge, IL

The dog tore my stockings, the garbagemen are on strike, and my hair's a mess. This would be a great day to go back to bed and pull the covers over my head! I'll try counseling tomorrow, when things are better.

But that's no good. Helping a client can't wait until my life is perfect. So here I am, looking into pain-filled eyes, trying to help someone get better.

For the next few hours, help me forget my problems. Help me do my job and just accommodate the voice reminding me we're out of bread and the freezer needs defrosting. Help me maintain my household and attend to my own chores while I balance my professional responsibilities.

Anonymous

"Depression is anger turned inward."

When I was a newcomer to this world of recovery, I believed my anger was a defect of character, a negative emotion. That I shouldn't even *get* angry.

Today I understand that anger is just another emotion, and to express anger in a healthy way is better for me than keeping it in. I'm no longer the perfect, always-kind person who doesn't show anger. And today, because of that, my kindness and concern for others is genuine. I can let them be human, because I've let myself be human.

Am I allowing myself to be a human being? Today, help me give those around me the freedom to express their anger without walking away or rejecting them.

V.B.
Park Ridge, IL

Helping a client recognize and heal shame is a big part of counseling. Shame is often exposed to us in the trivial: those moments when our guard is down and we feel less than adequate.

Counseling teaches me about my own shame, too. When I feel personally uncomfortable with any topic my client is sharing, my own shame raises its persistent head. I can heal my shame when I share the darkest parts of myself with *another*. Then I can find the human mirror of exposure and mutuality to reflect back to me a less shame-filled face.

"You can't kiss your own ear" is a Russian proverb. Today I will try to embrace my defects and to come to realize that *all* parts of me are beautiful, and I am not unique in the secrets I keep.

S.C.
Dowagiac, MI

When people are admitted for treatment or outpatient counseling, they have a lot of fear. This is a new and scary world. They want to change, to give up their addictions. But those chemicals have become their best friends. They haven't learned, yet, that chemicals will be replaced by something better.

Our reactions to a new client's fears is the first "test" we must pass, and it can make a difference in his or her recovery. They need to know we recognize their fears, and understand. That we take those feelings seriously. That we're willing to work hard to help.

Long before the first Twelve Step meeting, before the first group therapy session, before the first lecture, we can be ambassadors of good will to every new client. My prayer for today is that I be especially compassionate, that I acknowledge a new client's fears. Help me to show him that there can be a better life ahead.

Anonymous

This above all: to thine own self be true,
And it must follow, as night the day,
Thou canst not then be false to any man.

William Shakespeare

People-pleasing hurts me in so many ways. I don't like myself when I'm doing it. And it's a way of hiding from others; that's even worse. I begin to feel masked, that I've cloaked myself with the attitudes and beliefs of others in order to be accepted, or not make a fuss—but lost myself.

What a waste! The real "me" gets lost, buried beneath layers of smiling fakery. Who can love me as I really am, if I hide that person from sight? How can a person of integrity agree with everyone? How can I be honest with my clients if I'm lying to the world? Let me stop people-pleasing today. Help me to be true to myself. Give me the courage to trust that the world—and myself—will love me as I am.

Anonymous

To Love is to risk rejection
To Live is to risk dying
To Hope is to risk despair
To Try at all is to risk failure
But risk we must
Because the greatest hazard of all is risking nothing
Chained by his certitudes, one is a slave
Only a person who takes risks is free.

L.M.
Dallas, TX

I believe that God created people. I believe He could have made us like puppets on a string, that the greatest gift He gave us is the capacity to think and behave as we choose. If what I believe is true, then each person must be responsible for his own thoughts, feelings, and behavior. Help me to remember that I cannot be responsible for other peoples' thoughts, feelings, and behavior. Help me to understand that I cannot control the thoughts, feelings, and behavior of others. Help me to understand that the most I can do to help others is to be a role model and a mirror to others so that they may choose to change. Today, help relieve me of the belief that I should be responsible for changing someone other than myself.

L.W.
Austin, TX

Personality is not the product of one little lifetime. God has been at work for ages upon the personality of each of us through His great law of heredity. The result is that in all this world there are no two persons exactly alike—never have been and never will be.

What does this mean? You are God's opportunity in your day. He has waited ages for a person just like you. If you have yielded to Him and His will is being performed through you, then you are God's opportunity for change. If you refuse, God loses that opportunity. And He will never have another, for there will never be another person on earth just like you.

Today, let me make the most of my life. Let me truly be God's opportunity for goodness.

S.B.-P.
Houston, TX

Working in the field of addiction treatment and being a "recovering" person myself presents some unique problems to a professional's personal recovery program.

Working in the field is not a replacement for personal recovery needs. It will not substitute for going to a meeting, or active involvement in a program of recovery. Serving clients' needs all day doesn't fill my own recovery needs.

Because we spend many hours of our day talking about addiction, we may not want to go to a meeting and spend more time talking about our own addiction; that's understandable. But that feeling can be dangerous for our recovery if it takes us away from our regular meetings.

Working "in the field" grants no immunity from personal recovery needs. Am I keeping my own recovery program intact?

S.R.
Park Ridge, IL

Turn to prayer when angry, and learn tolerance for yourself and others.

Turn to prayer when frightened, and find courage.

Turn to prayer in grief, for the comfort of pain shared.

Turn to prayer in despair, and find hope for the future.

Turn to prayer when anxious, and discover inner peace.

Turn to prayer when defeated, and find the strength to try again.

Turn to prayer in loneliness, and learn you're not alone.

Turn to prayer in joy, to be one with your Higher Power.

Anonymous

When you've done all you can, but it isn't enough
—turn it over.

When the day's run out before the work is done—
turn it over.

When there's too much joy for one person to hold
—turn it over.

When the world seems a dreary and unhappy place
—turn it over.

When a loved one dies, and you can't let go—turn
it over.

When there's too much month at the end of the
money—turn it over.

When you long to escape, and relapse is near— turn
it over.

When you don't know which way to turn—turn it
over.

Today, let me remember: Let Go, Let God.

Anonymous

Sometimes we can't find the courage to stand on our feet until we get to our knees. Prayer helps us gather our inner resources, provides the strength we need to keep trying until we've solved a problem. In this sacred experience, we can open our hearts and admit our deepest feelings. Knowing a loving presence hears us, we can honestly petition help for our frailties and faults, our trial and troubles, our aims and ambitions. We can pour out our most deeply hidden feelings, our secrets and fears. On our knees, we rise far above everyday existence.

Today, let me not forget the power of prayer.

S.B.-P.
Houston, TX

There are days when my spirit feels dry. There are days when old wounds and hurts feel raw and new. There are days when my "special gifts" seem lost in the comings and goings of my busy world. There are days when good thoughts about myself feel locked in a box, and I'm without strength or the will to turn the key.

I'll be willing to let a dear and gentle friend become my key-turner. I'll risk asking for affirmation today. I'll take the risk of believing you, when I don't believe me.

Who will I invite "in" today?

S.C.
Dowagiac, MI

Life can be difficult. That's a given. And much of recovery depends on coming to accept this fact. Life is easier when our expectations are congruent with the realities of life. We must become willing to accept difficulty as part of the privilege of living. That's an indicator of developing maturity in a client . . . *AND* in a counselor.

Isn't it odd that so much of the essential skill a therapist can muster is based on such a simple spiritual tenet—"Life can be difficult"—and on a life-embracing spiritual response—"Let's get on with it."

Today, I ask my Higher Power to be with me. Please, grant me the wisdom to know your will for me and the power to carry that out.

J.S.
Rockford, IL

We're getting a new team member next week, and I hear she's enthusiastic, experienced, well-trained—in short, a terrific counselor. I can't wait to meet her and start working with her. It's so exciting to have someone new! Someone really competent to learn from, to rely on.

The counseling field may be unique in that we welcome expertise in our co-workers, even if it may overshadow our own. We need each other too much, depend on each other too much, to get caught up in petty jealousy and competition between ourselves. Our clients are a real challenge; we need all the help we can get to succeed in helping them.

I'm excited about this change in my work life. I give thanks today for a new team member who will teach, and learn, and be a comrade.

Anonymous

*Sometimes it's easier to learn about gratitude
outside under the stars.*

I overheard an old-timer at a support group meeting say, "I no longer have bad days." She went on to say that bad things still *happen* in her day, but she doesn't give anything the power to take her good day away.

Gratitude is a powerful attitude-changing drug. It's been called the surest antidote for the poison of self-pity. As a counselor, I recognize the curative powers of gratitude by observing my reaction to clients who are grateful and those that habitually complain. I feel hopeful and singing inside when I sit with a client whose basic attitude is gratitude. When I listen to the same problem from a client who's full of self-pity, the expectation of a joyous recovery is dulled. Luckily, miracles do happen, and wonderful attitude changes do regularly occur in many negative clients.

My insides can teach me a powerful lesson about my own level of gratitude, too. Do people usually sing inside when I'm around? Is my gratitude contagious? What am I grateful for today?

*S.C.
Dowagiac, MI*

Humility is realizing how much we need our Higher Power, which is often expressed through others in our lives. When first introduced to the word "humility," we may view it as being somewhere on a continuum, with a doormat at one end and bragging pride at the other. Chances are, people with true humility have more genuine self-esteem than those of us repeatedly attacked by pride. Humility is a tool which, like a pair of glasses, allows us to see correctly those forces which act within us, but which exist outside ourselves. Without this clarity, we may keep to a destructive course, since our behavior is colored by our past value system. We desperately need to remain aware of the world as it is, not distorted by the illusions of the past or the fears of the future. I'll trust that today is more than a sequence of coincidences. I'll greet all those entering my life, clients, new friends, and family, with an ever-growing awareness of their value and worth.

D.Y.
Austin, TX

*Be not angry that you cannot make others as you
wish them to be,
since you cannot make yourself as you wish to be.*

Thomas A'Kempis

The only person I can control is myself — yet
often I'm like a runaway train, chugging along, carrying emotions I don't want to feel, in the grip of
behavior I can't quite control, with a tangle of
thoughts careening through my mind like loose
change. At times like this, I'm most forgiving of my
clients. If I can't control my own life any better than
this, I surely have no business demanding more
from others!

Today, when I'm tempted to be critical and
out of sorts with others, I'll remember how my own
life goes out of control at times. I'll think about what
I need when I'm feeling that way. With God's
grace, I'll find ways to fill those needs in others, and
be tolerant and loving of all the "runaway trains" I
may meet.

Anonymous

Do I really believe that a good worker is someone who also knows how to have fun? How will I play and fit fun into my life today? Will it be a priority—or an afterthought? Some days I wonder how I ever got so serious! Every day, I need to work at changing.

I know I've gotten too serious when I find myself saying, "I don't have time for play, I have more important things to do." What could be more important than fun? It brings back perspective, helps me relax, gives me a break from thought. I'll work at making play a real part of my life. Today, I'll remember that sometimes, nothing is more important than fun.

S.C.
Dowaagiac, MI

An addiction counselor's worst enemy is denial. It makes clients over-protect themselves, hide who they really are, and resist our efforts to understand them. A client may reveal himself only for a moment, and never again. She may 'slip' and give vital information just once.

So, our communication systems must be very good. I must tell my team members what I observe, and clearly record the information for future use. And they must pass information along to me. How do we accomplish this? Only through paperwork. Charting. Progress notes. Shift logs. The work we often find so boring is, ironically, our best ally. The work we often do grudgingly, because it "interferes" with our client contact, may give us the key to breaking through a client's denial and helping them begin recovery.

When I'm impatient with paperwork, let me remember how important my information is to others. And as I read a years-old chart, let me be grateful to those who took the time and trouble to share their insights, and are helping me help my clients today.

K.I.
Chicago, IL

More and more, I need to find little islands of peace during my day. To avoid getting caught in a tornado of work that leaves me exhausted and tense, useless to myself and my clients. That's the start of self-pity, and I've learned to leave it be.

Instead, I'll take a walk at lunch, even if it's just around the block, even if it's raining. Between clients, I'll spend a few minutes thinking about my free time, when I have my own life. When things get unusually hectic, I'll take a few extra moments to wash my hands, comb my hair . . . anything to let go of tension and restore peace to my ruffled spirit.

These little islands of peace help keep me calm. I return to the work flurry feeling rested. Today, I'll find antidotes to burnout. I'll find ways to bring myself peace.

Anonymous

Prejudicial feelings toward a fellow human are a burden too heavy for me to bear. When I allow myself the grandiose belief that I'm better than someone else, then I must accept the awesome responsibility of proving that I'm better. This is one task I don't want, or need.

In many ways, I'm a product of my culture and environment, and as a result sometimes find prejudice raising its ugly head in my counseling sessions. Today, I believe I have the ability to identify and let go of those feelings, instead of holding onto them. The wise and effective counselors who have been my teachers and mentors strive for a sense of equality and human connection with their clients. Clients *always* know when they are looked down on or judged; growth and healing begin for them only when they feel safe and accepted by me.

Today, I'll seek supervision if I feel "better than" any client.

S.C.
Dowagiac, MI

I learned the value of Step One from a client in treatment. The client was an Eskimo, a double amputee. When 'surrender' was a topic in group therapy, he'd rap on his wooden legs and say, "When the doctor told me she amputated my legs, I didn't believe her, becuase it felt like they were still there. I wouldn't surrender."

How often in life I feel I'm in control, with the power to maneuver or manipulate a situation. How frequently I'm deluded enough to think I can help someone change if I'm just clever enough— and it always ends up in failure or disappointment. When that happens, I've lost track of the basic reality so necessary for success: "I am powerless."

J.B.
Pinellas Park, FL

No one likes to feel pain, even though it's necessary, signaling when something is wrong. But many addicted people have an excessive fear of pain and an almost automatic response: take a pill, have a drink, go to sleep, stuff yourself with food, stuff the feelings down—anything not to feel the hurt!

Recovery helps us learn that pain can be bearable, even useful. As we begin to recover, we look back and see that the times we've grown the most are the times when we've felt, accepted, and dealt with the most pain. We'll never come to look forward to pain—but we can stop running from it. We can learn that pain is less a problem when we confront it and share it with others.

Today I'll ask my Higher Power for the courage to walk through my pain instead of running away from it. I know I can reach out my hand and ask others to walk with me.

S.S.
Park Ridge, IL

When my clients relapse, it's always painful. I feel especially sad when someone with a lot of time in recovery relapses. Most clients experience terrible shame and loss of self-esteem when this happens.

This can be a time for some clients to do necessary grief work regarding losses, both real and imagined. A healing of memories needs to include a new belief: "I *made* a mistake;" not, "I *am* a mistake." Clients who feel shame and low self-worth often have great difficulty believing they deserve to live happily and fully. Some think they actually deserve to relapse. Let me help them believe in themselves, and love themselves enough to be happy.

S.C.
Dowagiac, MI

Nothing in life is to be feared
It is only to be understood.

Marie Curie

The hardest counseling days for me are the days when I'm so full of my own anxiety that I feel I have nothing to give. Days when I can't connect with my resources.

Acknowledging this feeling and saying a prayer for strength and guidance somehow get me through.

When I find my concentration drifting during sessions, I gently shift my focus back to my client, becoming willing to re-connect. Trusting that I will be given what I need in order to help my client has never failed me.

Personal anxiety is also my "teacher." I have learned to talk and write about my anxiety and fears, as a method of easing this personal pain.

I pray to be willing to accept my own brokenness as part of what makes me a human being and counselor.

S.C.
Dowagiac, MI

A newborn infant soon opens its eyes and begins to perceive the surrounding world. There is already an infantile knowledge of the need to be cared for. The newborn already knows that "no man is an island."

One in recovery, too, becomes aware of that gentle nudge toward maturity. The word "sanity" is from the Latin, *sanus,* which means soundness, health, integrity, wholeness. One comes to believe and rely on the fellowship of others in recovery, and a Higher Power who will administer loving care.

As one who counsels others, I must recognize my own need for help, faith, fellowship, and my Higher Power—the ultimate source of healing, sanity, integrity, and wholeness. Today, through my personal belief in a power greater than myself, I can be an instrument in the restoration of sanity for those who come to me.

J.B.
Pinellas Park, FL

I switched jobs recently, and the decision brought with it a multitude of feelings. For many days I had to harness my energy, excitement, and enthusiasm in order to cope with fear, doubt and insecurity. Immediately, I was rocketed into a different life with new faces, while the familar ones were left silently behind. "Courage to Change" was all I could recite in order to confront feelings of loneliness, anger, and emptiness. Everything seemed, just a short while ago, to be so positive. Then, some questions arose. What is my purpose? Is this what I want? Wait a minute . . . I must weigh my options, ask for direction, and begin with the support of others who seemed lost.

Now, slowly, the pieces are interlocking in a new life. Like a puzzle one walks away from out of frustration or boredom, then returns to, finding that a brief reprieve helped me complete another section. Finally, shape and form are apparent, bringing hope. Fresh, spring-morning smells finally greet me after what seemed to be unforgiving wintery winds that chapped, calloused, and caused pain. Today I will continue to realize my relationship with God.

J.G.
Chicago, IL

This day is too frantic, feelings are too intense, my spirit too troubled.

Just let me close my door on the distractions outside and around me for five minutes . . .

Five minutes just for me, to relax physically and emotionally and let serenity wash over me. The quiet renews and revitalizes me.

Just by affirming that I'm relaxed, I can handle anything with a peaceful demeanor. If I'm to be of any help to anyone today, I must remember to take myself to my quiet place.

V.B.
Park Ridge, IL

Mirth is like a flash of lightning, that breaks through
a gloom of clouds, and glitters for a moment;
cheerfulness keeps up a kind of daylight in the mind,
and fills it with a steady and perpetual serenity.

Joseph Addison

The counseling field has more than its fair share of comedians, which is lucky for us — nobody needs a laugh more than we do. There's usually someone to keep the tickle going, break up the somber seriousness of a hectic day with some much-needed fun. Someone who strung an entire box of paper clips into one long chain. The one with the big infectious laugh that booms into every corner of the office and sets everyone else smiling. Someone who always has a joke or funny story to share.

Today, I'm most grateful for team members who can make me laugh, and pray to have one on my shift.

Anonymous

Anticipation is a great motivator, so give yourself something pleasant to look forward to at the end of a day or a project. Looking forward brings renewed energy and zest for life. Plan ahead to celebrate the "ends" as much as the beginnings. Reward yourself with something special, even if it's just a few kind words from yourself—to yourself. Pat yourself on the back; praise yourself for the good job you did. Give yourself a night on the town, some quiet time, or a special gift. Looking forward to the end can help all of us get through the worst day.

What can I look forward to at the end of this day?

S.B.-P.
Houston, TX

It's the first day of winter with icicles starting, trees bowed with snow. Soon come the holidays, the season of giving, to brighten the world. The streets bustle with shoppers. Lawns are populated with snowmen, twinkled with colored lights. Friends and families reunited, young cheeks are pinched, cookies come smiling from the oven. The wind howls outside, but inside is warmth and love and generosity; inside, for this blessed season, we think more of others than ourselves.

What joy I have to share with my clients today! What energy to give: to lighten someone's burden just a little; to bring a message of peace and serenity to those around me.

Anonymous

Some must search for a way to give to those less fortunate. Others spend their lives trying to fill their days with useful, fulfilling tasks. I'm a counselor, so I'm lucky: All I have to do is go to work!

How blessed! Every day someone appears in my path who needs a helping hand, someone who needs a loving smile or a kind word, someone who needs education about their disease or "a little boot" to start them on the right path. Through my work, I can touch a life every day and experience the joy of recovery all over again. A career helping those in need can bring pain, that's true. But the joy far outweighs the grief.

Thank you for the privilege of touching a life each day.

K.H.
Austin, TX

Beauty is in the eye of the beholder.

William Shakespeare

If only I could help the person in front of me see the beauty that I see in them.

These addictions cloud our vision, dull our perceptions. Sometimes, it takes an outsider to put things in proper perspective. In sharing my own vision of beauty, I can offer a little hope to those who see none. And when my vision dims, someone in turn may share the beauty of his or her life with me.

I pray for help in keeping my eyes open to others' beauty, and my heart open to others' help.

V.B.
Park Ridge, IL

Who rises from prayer a better man,
his prayer is answered.

George Meredith

My child-prayers were for things like
a new bike
but no bike came.

Now I pray for strength
to accept what I have
and what will come.
My prayer is always answered.

Anonymous

Wouldn't it be wonderful if I could see again the things I saw when I was five or six years old?

A gander chasing a puppy dog. Great big watermelons, and corn stalks as high as the sky. Peach trees with a million peaches on every branch. And the spanking I got for picking some green ones. It amazed me to see those old, old 13- and 14-year-olds milking cows and plowing the fields. And how can I ever forget the beautiful look of love on my older brother's face when he pulled a sticker out of my foot?

Let me see these things again. Let me open my eyes and feel the love I had then for all things before me, even green peaches and a spanking. Today, thank You for sharing these things with me.

C.J.
Wilmer, TX

The love of praise, howe'er conceal'd by art,
Reigns more or less, and glows is ev'ry heart.

Edward Young

Good parents and good counselors know that praise accomplishes far more than criticism. It's easy for anyone to become hardened against criticism and ignore the message being delivered. But who can resist praise? Who can deny reality when reality comes in such a sweet package? It doesn't have to be elaborate or poetic; sincerity is the only requirement. Ah, praise . . . as wonderful to give as it is to get. Today, I'll give the gift of praise to myself and others.

Anonymous

Counseling and prayer go hand-in-hand for many of the counselors that I've met over the years. These counselors don't impose any spiritual or religious views onto their clients; they simply bring their own Higher Power into the counseling room with them. Counseling requires us to be open to the best and worst in others. It asks that we journey through deep pain, believing we will emerge whole and stronger on the other side. By its very healing nature, counseling is spiritual. When I have silently prayed to "bless the moment," I've felt a sense of renewed energy and direction in my sessions. Today I ask for my Higher Power's company in everything I do.

S.C.
Dowagiac, MI

Gentleness and dignity, kindness, and generosity of spirit are invisible except in action. It's easy to miss the inner beauty of those around us, to be misled by outside appearances. Finding that inner beauty in others takes effort, but the search is worthwhile. We look past clothing, physical attractiveness, worldly success, possessions, achievements —we look past the outer shell. Now, we're gazing into a soul, into the deepest reality of another. We see who someone *is*. How beautiful, how valiant, how dignified.

It's hard. I pray for the strength of character to put aside frivolous judgments. Help me to look deeply into every client I counsel, every stranger on the street, every beloved family member and friend. Grant me the love and serenity to find that inner beauty in everyone I meet.

K.I.
Chicago, IL

This is what it's all about! Yesterday I saw an ex-client, and he looks fantastic. It's been over a year since he graduated from treatment; I think he really made it this time. He's clean and prosperous, well-dressed, well-groomed. Best of all, he has a serene and loving look in his eyes.

What a fantastic experience for a counselor— to see a success, someone who is recovering from an addiction. The sight of him makes up for a lot of hard work, overtime, lost sleep, and worry during the times when I can't remember what it's all about.

I give great thanks today for being lucky enough to see this client. He's helped me remember why I love my work, why I wouldn't trade jobs with anybody. Today, I'll remember that it wasn't easy—but the good things never are.

Anonymous

What a piece of work is Man!
How noble in reason!
How infinite in faculty!
In form, in moving, how express and admirable!
In action, how like an angel!
In apprehension, how like a God!

William Shakespeare

How beautiful we human beings are—men, women; young, old; rich, poor; black white. Let me rejoice in my humanity. Help me to find glory in all the things I am, and all you are. Let me love myself and others as we are, yet always strive to be more.

As this year comes to an end, let me give thanks for what I've accomplished. Let me learn from my mistakes, yet forgive myself for making them.

And let me look forward to a new year with excitement, serenity, and joy.

Anonymous

Index

Other meditation books that will interest you . . .

Each Day a New Beginning
Daily Meditations for Women
The first daily meditation guide created by and for women involved in Twelve Step recovery programs. Hundreds of thousands of women have found help in this collection of thoughts and reflections that offer hope, strength, and guidance every day of the year. 400 pp.
Order No. 1076

Touchstones
A Book of Daily Meditations for Men
Created especially for men in recovery, this daily meditation guide offers insight into emotions, becoming whole people, finding spiritual enlightenment, masculinity, anger, communication and sexuality, among many other topics. *Touchstones* possesses a rare blend of inspiration and contemplation that will touch any man involved in a Twelve Step program. 400 pp.
Order No. 5029

For price and order information, or a free catalog, please call our Telephone Representatives.

HAZELDEN

1-800-328-0098   **1-651-213-4000**   **1-651-213-4590**
(24-Hour Toll Free.   (Outside the U.S.   (24-Hour FAX)
U.S., Canada, and the   and Canada)
Virgin Islands)

Pleasant Valley Road • P.O. Box 176 • Center City, MN 55012-0176
www. hazelden. org